IMAGES
of Sport

SWINTON

RUGBY LEAGUE FOOTBALL CLUB

CW00504729

Albert Blan receives the Rugby League Championship Trophy in 1963, a feat he was to repeat twelve months later.

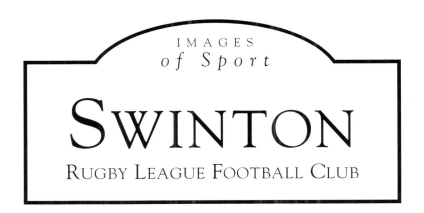

IMAGES
of Sport

SWINTON

RUGBY LEAGUE FOOTBALL CLUB

Stephen Wild

TEMPUS

Dedication

This book is dedicated to Lesley, Hayley, Stevie, Katie, and all my friends connected with Swinton Lions.

First published 2002
Copyright © Stephen Wild, 2002

Tempus Publishing Limited
The Mill, Brimscombe Port,
Stroud, Gloucestershire, GL5 2QG

ISBN 0 7524 2708 3

TYPESETTING AND ORIGINATION BY
Tempus Publishing Limited
PRINTED IN GREAT BRITAIN BY
Midway Colour Print, Wiltshire

Introduction

In October 1866, a group of bored middle-class cricketers decided to play 'football' on Saturday afternoons to pass away the tedious winter months. They were the village of Swinton's privileged young men, since the majority of the 8,000 or so other inhabitants would spend their own Saturdays earning a meagre subsistence slaving in a cotton mill or down a pit. But when government legislation allowed the working classes the opportunity of a half-day Saturday, how Swinton's villagers embraced this so-called invigorating sport!

As members of the Rugby Football Union (RFU) right from its year of inception (1871), Swinton could call upon the best players from numerous feeder clubs. It seemed as if every young man in the area wanted to play rugby football, and so the 'Lions' were able to progress from strength to strength in a remarkably short period of time. The club achieved national notoriety despite the snobbery and prejudices of a pompous RFU and despite the sarcastic tag of the 'oft sneered at colliery village club'.

Although the very flagship of the RFU in Lancashire, Swinton belatedly joined the fledgling rebel breakaway (entitled the Northern Rugby Football Union) in 1896. The loss of too many close geographical rivals a year earlier provided the financial catalyst that ensured a reluctant defection. By now Swinton's population had swelled, but the town's love affair with rugby football continued in earnest. Crowds approaching 20,000 – at a time when the population was only 30,000 – flooded into the Chorley Road ground as the Lions reached their zenith between 1925 and 1928.

Despite its proximity to Manchester (about four-and-a-half miles), Swinton had been an inaccessible Lancashire outpost in the late nineteenth century but, as the twentieth century progressed, the town slowly became more and more engulfed by the ever-expanding conurbation. Still it retained its proud independence, and any native Swintonian or Pendlebury man will tell you that the town is historically and geographically quite distinct from Salford, despite what modern-day politicians might have you believe and despite the unpopular imposition of the Maud Report on, appropriately, April Fool's Day 1974. Salford's background was altogether different: an economy and population connected with the heavy industry of the docks and the ship canal, as opposed to Swinton's colliers and millers. In the old days, they had local derbies that would make a modern Saints versus Wigan clash resemble a convent tea-party.

A renaissance for the Lions in the mid-1960s was followed by a dramatic fall in fortunes over the next twenty-five years. This terrible decline ultimately led the club to betray its greatest asset – the famous Station Road ground. This was closely followed by an even greater betrayal – that of the very game itself, with the advent of 'Super League'.

Hitherto, and for all of 100 years, the Rugby League had been a close-knit family of clubs that had survived the worst of the Establishment's discrimination and two world wars. It was a sport steeped in tradition and a sense of belonging: Mount Pleasant, Batley; Crown Flatt, Dewsbury; Craven Park, Barrow; Watersheddings, Oldham; Station Road, Swinton; and many others. Just simply saying those names used to be enough to make you push your chest out with pride, as the hairs on the back of your neck stood on end. These are not just Rugby League clubs, they are time-honoured institutions. This unique sport even permeated into the everyday dialect of these proud northern towns. Certainly in Swinton if something was deemed 'good' (applying to anything and everything), then it was said to be 'the finest in the Northern Union'. My own grandmother used this phrase quite often without, I'm sure, ever realising its origins.

So what have we got now? Sky TV and 'Murdoch's millions' the saviours of the game? I think not. One or two of the very top sides might have done alright out of it (so far), but just look at the state of the clubs in the Northern Ford Premiership. Look what happened to Bramley, and what about York? Check out the dire finances of other once proud clubs, for goodness sake look at Swinton! Can virtually every club in the division be blamed for its own current crisis, or is there something fundamentally wrong with the organisation of the sport? Clubs like Swinton are hanging on by their bootlaces, whilst other clubs – in the fortunate position of having been in the right place at the right time – cock a snoop as the game reels in its own heartlands.

Super League has ignored the value of tradition in Rugby League and the chickens are coming home to roost. How many traditional clubs folded pre-Super League? How many championships have Swinton won and how many, for example, have Castleford won? If the answers are not obvious, then please check your yearbooks. Then what of our more privileged neighbours? Bradford using a portion of their 'Sky money' to rally for support in Batley, and Salford likewise in Swinton. Not illegal, of course, but somehow distasteful and against the spirit of brotherhood and mutual survival that used to exist amongst Rugby League clubs.

But perhaps there is a way forward for clubs outside the top division (other than the rightful goal of automatic promotion) and perhaps part of the answer is to go back to the beginning of rugby history. Members' clubs, democratically controlled by anyone wishing to play an active part – be they a player, a businessperson or an average supporter – but with certain attitudes in common. A genuine love for the club and its traditions, and a deep awareness of the club's responsibility to the community it is supposed to represent. On too many occasions in recent years, the directors (of our limited liability companies) have seemingly shown scant regard for the fact that they were merely privileged and temporary custodians of a crucial part of their town's heritage. Indeed, as we have seen at several clubs of late, far too many officials are inclined to embark on ego trips and simply do not understand the deep-rooted cultural factors that commit people to support Rugby League clubs.

At Swinton, a 'Supporters Trust' was formed in the spring of 2002. It has a dual motto: 'Let those who pay have a say' and 'For club and for community'. A democratic partnership of officials, supporters and the community is surely the most sensible route to take. For more details, go to www.lionstrust.co.uk or send an s.a.e. to 70 Swinton Hall Road, Swinton, Manchester M27 4BJ.

The only hope for Swinton is that it's not too late. Hopefully, the recent relocation to Moor Lane will be regarded as a step in the right direction and encourage better support. Having been distanced from its own community for ten years will no doubt prove a huge burden to overcome, as will a more cosmopolitan population and a tendency for today's youngsters to worship the round ball rather than the oval one. But whilst there are people who have a genuine passion, there will always be a chance. Perhaps after reading this book and looking through the historical images, it will stir the emotions and encourage people to come forward and get behind the Swinton Supporters Trust. Don't leave it to somebody else. This book will not only demonstrate that Swinton has a history worth preserving, but that it also deserves a future.

Stephen Wild,
Swinton, 2002.

The White Lion in Swinton, built in 1790, is synonymous with the history of the club. Although Swinton's original headquarters were at the Bull's Head, by 1873 they had moved to the White Lion and a famous nickname, 'The Lions', was born. The name stuck despite the fact that the club reverted back to the Bull's Head in 1898.

William Longshaw was a wealthy cotton-mill owner and church warden. He resided at the impressive Swinton Hall, which once stood on the site of the present-day shopping precinct. He was the driving force behind the formation of the Lions, and his sons, Walter and Harry, were Swinton's first captains. Longshaw remained club president from the time Swinton joined the Rugby Football Union in 1871 until his death in 1888. Meanwhile, Walter, along with Herbert 'Buck' Farr, became the first Lions to win representative honours when they played for Lancashire against Yorkshire at Halifax in January 1878.

This aerial view of Swinton town centre helps pinpoint the exact position of Swinton's Stoneacre pitch (i.e. at the point where Lions Drive – the newer houses – merges into Bingham Street). The houses at the bottom left-hand corner cover the site of the old Swinton cricket ground. The Lions' Chorley Road ground (home from 2 October 1886 to 1929) lay just out of the photograph, to the left of the former cricket ground.

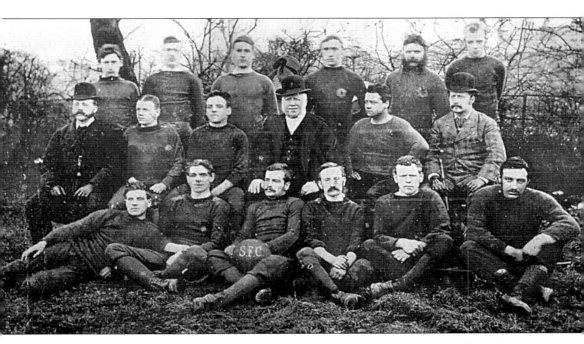

The first known group photograph of a Swinton team, taken in 1876, in the middle of a run which saw the Lions remain undefeated for three entire seasons. It was probably taken on the Stoneacre ground, where the Lions played between 1873 and 1886. From left to right, back row: Herbert Farr, Henry Farr, Edward Farr, George Townsend, William Evans, Ted Barker. Middle row: Radcliffe Dorning (umpire), John Dorning, Bob Ogden, William Longshaw (president), Arthur Dorning, Harry Longshaw (umpire). Front row: R. Ashton, Tom Morrison, Walter Longshaw (captain), John Owen, James Barlow, Tom Clegg.

Former track sprinter Ted Beswick, who joined the Lions in 1879, became Swinton's first international footballer when he was selected to play for England against Ireland in Dublin on 4 February 1882. A month later, he earned a second cap against Scotland at Whalley Range. A tricky three-quarter and resolute tackler, Beswick captained the Lions during 1880/81 and 1881/82. He also appeared once for the North and scored 4 tries in 5 appearances for Lancashire.

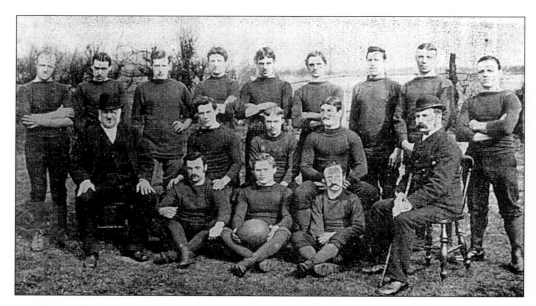

A sensational victory over Manchester in March 1878 was a defining moment in the club's history and, by 1881, the Lions had become renowned as the best team in Lancashire. From the autumn of 1878, they had been seeking adversaries from across the Pennines, such as Wakefield Trinity, Halifax, Bradford, Kirkstall and Dewsbury. From left to right, back row: Ted Barker, Billy Howarth, John Seddon, Charlie Horley, Harry Hope, Albert Hope, Bob Seddon, Jack Cheetham, Bob Ogden. Middle row: William Longshaw (president), Walter Bumby, Billy Cooke, Tom Farr, Walter Longshaw (umpire). Front row: Joe Mills, Ted Beswick (captain), John Owen.

Tom Farr (pictured) was one of four brothers to play for the Lions in the early days. Sons of the local physician, each made their mark on the club. Herbert was the star of the 1870s and, on one occasion, scored five tries in a game to set a record that was not beaten until 1996. Edward was heavily involved on the club's committee from its inception, Henry became secretary in 1876, whilst Tom held the captaincy in seasons 1879/80 and 1883/84 and gained 5 caps for Lancashire.

Between October 1880 and November 1885, the Lions completed 63 matches undefeated at their Stoneacre home. At this time, the strongest team in England were reputed to be the Oxford University club, so when the Lions were invited south for a fixture, there could be no doubting that Swinton had achieved a reputation of national proportions. On 12 February 1883, the Lions lost by a single disputed converted try, but this remained their only defeat of the entire season. From left to right, back row: Albert Hope, Nathan Hotchkiss, Bob Seddon, John Seddon, Billy Howarth, Harry Hope, Charlie Horley, Walter Dickinson, Bob Ogden. Middle row: Ross Andrew (financial secretary), Fred Grover (umpire), Tom Banks, Ted Beswick, Tom Farr, William Longshaw (president). Front row: Billy Cooke, Joe Mills (captain), Walter Bumby. No less than twelve of these players gained county honours with Lancashire.

Nathan Hotchkiss was a robust forward who stood no nonsense on the field. He was also a loyal servant to the Lions, and became the first Swinton player to achieve 300 appearances. He won 9 caps for Lancashire between 1886 and 1889.

Charlie Horley was perhaps the finest forward of the Lions' Rugby Union days. His Swinton career spanned the years 1879 to 1893, during which time he won 20 Lancashire caps and appeared 3 times for the North. On 7 February 1885, he became the Lions' second England international when he played against Ireland.

Another England international was full-back Sam Roberts, pictured here (in later life) on the cover of a 1927 programme. Roberts was a renowned sportsman, who came to Swinton from the Bury club in 1885. Roberts made an immediate impact and, in December 1886, played at full-back for the North against the South at Blackheath. Following a fine performance in this trial match, he gained international caps against Wales and Ireland in early 1887. He also played 7 times for Lancashire.

On 12 March 1887, Lancashire met Middlesex at the Kennington Oval to mark Queen Victoria's Golden Jubilee. Three Swinton men were chosen to play in this prestigious match in front of a 12,000 crowd which included the Prince of Wales. Sam Roberts is pictured fifth from the left (standing), whilst Joe Mills and and the legendary Jim Valentine are seated next to each other on the right. England international Robert Seddon (seated far right) would controversially join Swinton shortly afterwards from Broughton Rangers.

A Baines card commemorating the ill-fated Robert Seddon. In the summer of 1888, a 'rebel' group became the first rugby tourists to leave these shores for Australia and New Zealand. Four Swinton men were involved: Arthur Paul, Walter Bumby, Tom Banks and Seddon, who was elected captain. However, on 4 August 1888, he tragically lost his life in a boating accident on the River Hunter near Maitland, New South Wales at the age of just twenty-seven.

Jim Valentine was arguably the most famous 'Lion' of all-time. First spotted whilst playing for Brindle Heath at the age of fourteen, 'Val' made his Swinton debut on 5 January 1884 against Walton at the age of seventeen. Whilst still only eighteen, he made an inauspicious debut for his county, but happily this did not prevent him from going on to secure a staggering 58 Lancashire RU caps, to which he added another 5 under the auspices of the Northern Union. He was capped by England in 1890, and played in all three Triple Crown matches during the 1895/96 season. His finest moment came sixteen years after his debut, when, aged almost thirty-four, he captained Swinton to a Challenge Cup final victory over bitter rivals Salford. Such were his services to both codes that he became the first Rugby player ever to be awarded a testimonial and, by the time he retired, he had amassed a record (by a clear 101) 298 tries for the Lions, for whom he had made 481 appearances – a total exceeded only by Ken Gowers. His 48 try haul in season 1888/89 remains a club record to this day. However, he was tragically to meet an untimely end.

England line up at Dewsbury for the match against Wales on 15 February 1890. Making his international debut is Jim Valentine (seated second from the right on the middle row). Andrew Stoddart of Blackheath is the captain with the ball, with whom the working-class Valentine did not see eye to eye.

Another major star of Swinton's Rugby Union era was Walter Bumby. He captained the Lions during 1889/90 and 1892/93, and gained 23 caps for Lancashire. He also toured Australasia with the 1888 rebels. In an era of southern bias, an international appearance eluded him, although he did play once for the North in February 1890. For the Lions he contributed to a much celebrated half-back partnership alongside Joe Mills. After retiring, he ran the Bridgewater Arms in Pendlebury for thirty years.

Joe Mills was not only a great servant of the Swinton club, but also of the town itself. A highly respected half-back, whose achievements were perhaps only overshadowed by Jim Valentine, he gained 29 Lancashire caps, made 2 appearances for the North, was twice named reserve for England, and captained Lancashire during 1889/90. His Swinton playing career spanned seventeen years, but he also served as secretary, county representative and club president. Away from rugby, he enjoyed periods as landlord of both the Bull's Head and the Football Hotel and, amongst countless other roles, he served as a local councillor for twenty years and as a Justice of the Peace. He died in 1920 following an appendicitis operation.

In 1890/91, Lancashire won ten matches out of ten to break Yorkshire's stranglehold on the County Championship. The captain, Jim Valentine, is pictured with the ball, whilst Swinton forward Tom Rothwell is standing second from the left on the back row. This photograph was taken prior to a challenge match against the Rest of England, which was narrowly lost at Whalley Range in front of an 18,000 crowd. Other Swinton men to appear for the county during this season were Walter Bumby and James Marsh.

❖ Teams. ❖
·········

LANCASHIRE.	YORKSHIRE.
BACK.	**BACK.**
J. Boscow (Warrington).	G. Lorimer (Manningham).
THREE-QUARTER BACKS.	**THREE-QUARTER BACKS.**
W. McCutcheon (Oldham).	R. E. Lockwood (Heckmondwike).
J. Marsh (Swinton).	A. Goldthorpe (Hunslet).
D. C. Woods (Manchester).	J. Dyson (Huddersfield).
HALF BACKS.	**HALF-BACKS.**
W. Parlane (Manchester Rangers).	J. Briggs (Bradford).
W. Bumby (Swinton).	H. Duckett (Bradford).
FORWARDS.	**FORWARDS.**
T. Case (Ulverston).	J. Toothill (Bradford).
S. Pierce (Liverpool).	H. Bradshaw (Bramley).
E. King (Salford).	D. Jowett (Heckmondwike).
V. Atkinson (Wigan).	E. Redman (Manningham).
T. Mellodew (Rochdale Hornets).	W. Lorryman (Leeds).
J. Jolley (Warrington .	M. Fletcher (Leeds).
J. P. Wilson (Liverpool Old Boys).	J. Bradley (Bradford).
T. Kent (Salford).	H. Speed (Castleford).
T. Rothwell (Swinton).	C. Richardson (Leeds Parish Church).

Referee: A. R. DON WAUCHOPE, Esq. (Scottish Union.)

L. & Y.

GRAND HOTEL, MANCHESTER.
Saturday, Nov. 26th 1892.

A dinner reception for the 'Roses' teams was held at Manchester's Grand Hotel following a drawn game in November 1892. James Marsh, who also had the unique distinction of winning international caps with both England and Scotland, captained Lancashire on this occasion.

In 1892/93, the RFU formed County Leagues in Lancashire and Yorkshire in an effort to placate disgruntled northern clubs. This is the Swinton team that finished runners-up in the Lancashire Senior Competition in both 1892/93 and 1893/94. From left to right, back row: Alf Sharples, Harold Murray, Sam Hall, Tom Hallam, Charlie Horley, Tom Rothwell, W. Chapman. Middle row: Jack Lewis, Herbie Brockbank, Jim Valentine, Walter Bumby, Bill Winterbottom, Billy Pearson. Front row: Nat Hotchkiss, George Sharples.

REPRESENTATIVE RUGBY CLUBS. No. 4—SWINTON.

This artistic illustration appeared in a popular magazine called *The Million* in 1893.

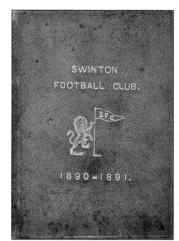  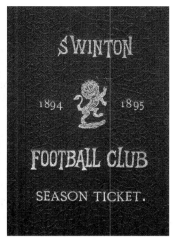

These season ticket books of 1890/91, 1891/92 and 1894/95 list (amongst others) adversaries such as Swansea, Manchester, Cardiff, Newport, Liverpool Old Boys, the Barbarians, Moseley, Llanelly, Leicester, Exeter, Devonport Albion, Oxford University, Hartlepool Rovers and Bristol. The calibre of this fixture list goes some way towards explaining why Swinton did not become founder members of the Northern Union in August 1895. Only the financial impact of losing big local fixtures was to force their hand and, on 7 May 1896, the Lions were formally admitted to the Northern Union.

Fred Grover succeeded William Longshaw as club president in 1888 and, in 1890, he became president of the Lancashire RFU. As a staunch Union man, he was vehemently opposed to the Lions joining the breakaway league and resigned his membership of the club when that path was taken following a vote at Swinton's AGM on 30 April 1896.

19

John Bowden was club president from 1890 until his death in 1896. It was Bowden's financial generosity that ensured that Swinton survived their last year as members of the RFU and were able to take up a new lease of life under the new order.

The Lions made an early impact in the Northern Union, and recruited widely from South Wales amidst rumours that they paid the highest wages in the fledgling code. Pictured in 1898/99 are, from left to right, back row: J. Reynolds, Jack Preston, George Harris. Second back row: Joe Mills (secretary), Jack Evans, Jim Worthington, Bob Tickle, Jim Shepherd, Evan Vigors, Jack Johnson, Ross Andrew (president). Seated: Bobby Messer, Owen Badger, Jim Valentine (captain), Jack Lewis, Morgan Bevan. Front row: Billy Pearson, Jonty Goodman, Joey Morgan.

Bill Widdowson gave loyal service to the Lions over many years in various offices, including honorary treasurer from 1896 and then club president between 1898 and 1900.

Ross Andrew was the honorary financial secretary in the latter years of the Lions' membership of the Rugby Union. He became club president after John Bowden's death and was renowned for his sense of humour, often introducing financial statements with tongue-in-cheek speeches regarding their authenticity!

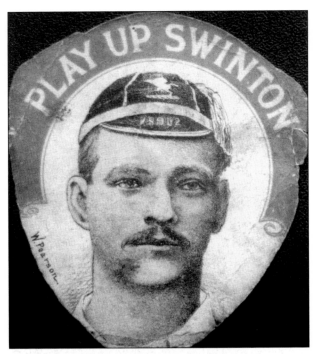

Billy Pearson, featured here on another Baines card, was a top-class half-back who won 3 caps for Lancashire under the RFU and another under the Northern Union. He scored a drop-goal in Swinton's first ever game as members of the Northern Union (a 17-6 success over Warrington at Chorley Road) and was elected captain at the start of the 1899/1900 season. However, after soon losing his place to Joey Morgan, he became so disillusioned that he vowed never to play for the Lions again. The ageing Valentine was reinstated as skipper and went on to lead his team to glory. Pearson's son, Jack, was the Lions' full-back during the halcyon days of the late 1920s.

Swinton should have contested the first ever Challenge Cup final, but were surprisingly beaten by underdogs St Helens in the semi-final of 1897. However, three years later, the Lions did reach the final in which they faced none other than arch-rivals Salford. Along the route Eastmoor, Holbeck, Oldham, Broughton Rangers and Leeds Parish Church were defeated, and then the final was won 16-8 at Fallowfield. The ground existed as an athletics track until fairly recently when it was built over. Here the author's daughter, Hayley, stands outside Fallowfield's bricked-up turnstiles shortly before its demolition in 1994.

This is the very medal that was won by Dick Jones, a forward in Jim Valentine's victorious 1900 Challenge Cup final team. This extremely rare item is 18ct gold and is suitably engraved on its reverse.

Jack Scholes was a loyal club man of many years standing. He was one of the original directors when the club became a limited company in 1904, and was often handed the precarious and dangerous task of travelling to South Wales to secure new talent for the Lions – amongst them Dai Davies.

Collecting trade cards was as popular with youngsters at the turn of the twentieth century as it is now. At this time, Baines of Bradford produced packs of six cards which sold for a halfpenny.

Copyright   Hampson, Ltd., Pendlebury

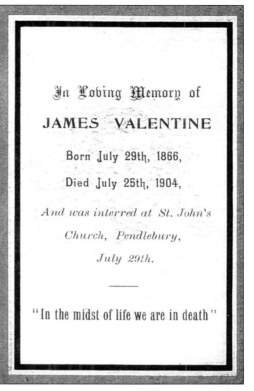

In Loving Memory of

JAMES VALENTINE

Born July 29th, 1866,

Died July 25th, 1904,

And was interred at St. John's

Church, Pendlebury,

July 29th.

———

"In the midst of life we are in death"

Having retired from first-team football in 1901, Jim Valentine remained with the Lions as a member of the management committee. In 1904, Valentine was due to take his seat on the newly formed board of directors. However, that summer he and his wife had gone on a week's holiday to Barmouth in North Wales where, on 19 July, he was enjoying a walk along a hilltop path. Suddenly they were caught up in the midst of a violent thunder storm, during which Valentine was struck down and killed instantly by lightning. He had been due to return home just a few hours later. Valentine's funeral took place at St John's church in Pendlebury, on what would have been his thirty-eighth birthday. The crowd was said to have stood six ranks deep from his home, the Duchy Arms at Brindle Heath, to the churchyard. The entire football world was devastated by this extraordinary loss of a legendary sportsman.

FOOTBALL CLUB STAND ON FIRE.

DAMAGE OVER £500.

The principal stand for spectators on the ground of the Swinton Football Club was totally destroyed by fire on Thursday night. Twice each week during the football season, on Tuesday and Thursday nights, the players are in the habit of turning out for practice, the ground on these occasions being illuminated by means of a number of Wells' lights. These lights are naked and wide-spreading, and although there is a space of several yards between the line along which they are fixed and it is supposed that the flame which set the structure on fire came from one of them. In what manner communication was effected, however, is a mystery. For the purpose of the usual practice the lights were set going shortly after half-past six, and the first symptom of the impending conflagration was observed a few minutes before seven. By this time many of the players, together with several officials of the club, had entered the inclosure, and naturally they were startled to see flame and smoke issuing from the centre of the stand, where the fire appears to have originated. This of course brought the rehearsal to an abrupt conclusion. An alarm was raised, and in a few minutes the volunteer fire brigade of the district, whose headquarters are close at hand, were in attendance and attacking the fire with a couple of jets attached to the street mains. At the same time a telephone message was sent to Salford requesting the attendance of the borough brigade. This was received at the Chief Fire Station in Ford-street at three minutes past seven, and a detachment with tenders and an escape reached the scene of the fire 15 minutes later, only to find the stand a seething mass of flame, the glare of which could be seen plainly from Pendleton, Eccles, Higher Broughton and other places for miles round. The new arrivals added several jets to those already in use, and after about an hour's energetic work the fire was extinguished, but not before the whole of the woodwork entering into the composition of the stand and a considerable length of hoarding had been consumed. Absolutely nothing was left standing except the brick supports. Mr. Cooper, the trainer for the club, narrowly escaped injury from falling timber whilst making an attempt to recover some personal property from the storeroom underneath the stand. Amongst the property of the club destroyed were some sixty sacks containing spent hops for covering the field of play as a protection against frost. Large numbers of people were attracted by the great blaze to the vicinity of the ground, and not a little excitement prevailed amongst the residents in the streets adjoining the field. The stand which has been destroyed was erected some years ago, during the secretaryship of Mr. Murray, at a cost of about £600. Fortunately for the club the damage is covered by insurance. No time will be lost in putting up a new stand, and there will be no suspension of play in the meantime.

In November 1901, Swinton's main stand (which had been built at great expense in 1890) was totally consumed by fire. This event perhaps marked the beginning of a period spanning some eighteen years, during which the club lurched from one financial disaster to another.

A Swinton team group *c*. 1906. The captain, Jack Evans, is the big man with the moustache stood in the middle of the second-to-back row. Elusive half-back and great Welsh playmaker Dai Davies is seated crosslegged on the left. Both men played in the 1900 cup-winning team, and indeed Davies holds the unique distinction of having also played in an FA Cup final (for Bolton Wanderers in 1904). Evans is the older half of a unique father and son double, who have both won Challenge Cups with the Lions. Jack junior was successful in 1926 and again in 1928.

Following the demise in 1909 of three Welsh Northern Union clubs – Barry, Treherbert and Aberdare – full-back Gordon Thomas was recruited from the latter.

Under the captaincy of Dai Davies, in December 1910, the Lions reached their first major final since 1900. However, despite scoring the only try of the game through winger Tommy Gartrell, Swinton were defeated 4-3 by Oldham in the Lancashire Cup final at Wheater's Field, Broughton. Tom McVeigh, pictured here, played in the forwards.

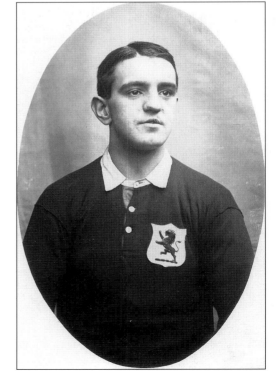

Frank Moores was a prolific try-scorer for the Lions in the period immediately before the First World War. From season 1912/13, he was the club's top try-scorer for three consecutive seasons with 15, 16 and 9 respectively. During 1912/13, he also won 2 caps for Lancashire. He served in the armed forces and survived the war, making a further 5 appearances in the 1919/20 season.

QUALITY VALUE

WEAR
FRED WOOD'S
Hats & Caps
••••••••••
the Latest Styles. .

Directly opposite Station,
HUDDERSFIELD.

years with Messrs. Garrett & Haigh.

Marsland & Sons,

BREWERS
of the well-known

ARKLING BOTTLED ALE
and
Invalid Stout.

Always reliable.
Always in first-class condition.

ATERGATE BREWERY,
HUDDERSFIELD.

erything in Men's Wear,
POPULAR PRICES
AT
H. LAYCOCK,
9, Cross Church St.,
HUDDERSFIELD. . .

"UP-TO-DATE" Hosier and Hatter.

6-50.   **Palace.**   9-0.

TO-NIGHT !   TO-NIGHT !

Violet Black & Co.,   The Martelloni Family.
in
SCREAMINGLY FUNNY SKETCH   **S. W. WYNDHAM,** Comedian.
"IN THE TUBE."   *And GRAND STAR COMPANY.*

NEXT WEEK - LADY LITTLE, THE DOLL LADY.

VISIT THE PALACE !   **GET THE HABIT !**

HUDDERSFIELD	G	T	SWINTON	G	T
SELECTED FROM			SELECTED FROM		
BACK—			FULL BACK—		
17 M. Holland ..			1 E. D. Griffiths ..		
THREE QUARTERS—			THREE QUARTERS—		
2 A. Rosenfeld ..			2 A. Morris ..		
3 E. Wrigley ..			3 M. Ryder ..		
4 H. Wagstaff, captain			4 J. D. Wharton ..		
16 S. Moorhouse ..			5 A. Valentine ..		
5 W. F. Kitchen ..			6 J. B. Parker ..		
HALF BACKS—			HALF BACKS—		
7 T. H. Grey ..			7 Dai. Davies, captain		
6 J. Davies ..			8 J. W. Fairhurst ..		
FORWARDS—			FORWARDS—		
9 C. A. Byrne ..			9 J. E. Blears ..		
10 D. Clark ..			10 Dan Davies ..		
11 B. Gronow ..			11 T. Gartrell ..		
8 J. Higson ..			12 T. J. McVeigh ..		
12 F. Longstaffe ..			14 W. Preston ..		
13 H. Sherwood ..			15 R. Price ..		
14 H. Walton ..			16 C. Randell ..		

Touch Judges—S. Mortimer, Dewsbury
E. J. Kilvington, Leeds

Referee—MR. W. McCUTCHEON, Oldham

CLUB NOTICES.   FOOTBALL AT FARTOWN.
Wed., Feb. 21st—Huddersfield v. HUNSLET.   3-30
Sat. Feb. 24th—Hudd. Reserves v. Oldham Reserves   3-30
„ March 2nd—Huddersfield v. BRAMLEY   3-30

After the Match
Call at **Rushworth's,** (Opposite Fox & Grapes Inn).

VALUE IN BOOTS, 6/11, 8/11, 10/6. Style and Wear.

We don't sell Hats,   **Busy Boot Makers,**
But we "cap" you with Boots.   **2, Bradford Road.**

ESTABLISHED 1852
Fillans & Sons,
Practical
WATCHMAKERS AND JEWELLERS,
Market Walk, Huddersfield,
have a Fine Stock of every description of
English and Foreign Watches, from
10/6 to £30.
Their Stock of Fancy Jewellery, Diamond
Rings, Guards, Alberts, etc., etc.,
is well assorted and at Reasonable Prices.

Fillans & Sons' Workshops are well known in the District
for Efficiency and Moderate Charges.

Telephone No. 312.

SETH SENIOR & SONS,

Brewers,
Wine and Spirit
Merchants,
and Mineral Water
Manufacturers.

ORDER OFFICE AND STORES:—

SUN BUILDINGS,
CROSS CHURCH ST.
HUDDERSFIELD,
AND
Highfield Brewery, Shepley.

GARRETT & HAIGH,
The Hatters,
27, New St., Huddersfield.

Oldest established Hatters in Huddersfield.

Sole Agents for the celebrated **TWEEN**
HATS.
MADE IN HALF SIZES.

This is the line-up for Swinton's unenviable Challenge Cup tie at Huddersfield on 17 February 1912. For the last time in twenty-eight years, the name Valentine appears in Swinton colours (Jim's brother, Albert), whilst for the famous 'Team of all the Talents', note the names of Albert Rosenfield, Harold Wagstaff and Ben Gronow, amongst many others. The Lions lost the game 30-0.

29

Dai Davies came to Swinton as an eighteen-year-old reserve international half-back in 1899, having apparently signed a hastily-prepared contract on a shop window in South Wales. He was a try-scorer in the victorious 1900 Challenge Cup final and, for three seasons, formed a superb partnership with his fellow countryman Joey Morgan. After a spell as goalkeeper for Bolton Wanderers between 1902 and 1909, he returned to captain the Lions, and was even selected for Wales when they faced England in December 1910. He served with the Swinton Pals during the First World War, after which he was involved with the Swinton Park amateur club.

Jim Pollitt's career was also disrupted by the war, and whilst not the most famous player of his day, his Swinton career (which spanned thirteen years from 1908 onwards) deserves recognition. 1916 was an eventful year for Pollitt. He played for the Lancashire League against the Yorkshire League in April but, later in the year, he was pulled from the water after his troopship had been torpedoed by a German U-boat! Along with Jack Bailey, he was awarded a benefit match in February 1922.

Jack Bailey's experience as a champion boxer often proved useful on the rugby field, and he was perhaps Swinton's most influential forward during the years surrounding the First World War. Before the war, he scored 2 tries in 2 appearances for Lancashire and, in 1920, he narrowly missed selection for the Great Britain tour of Australasia. In April 1916, he had a remarkable escape with his life after being shot clean through the chest by a machine-gun bullet whilst serving in the trenches on the Western Front.

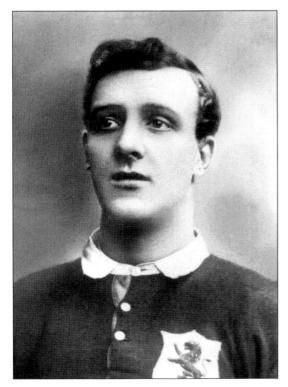

Matt Ryder was a local man and a hugely popular player of his day. He broke into the team in 1911/12, and could play full-back or centre. He was also an expert goalkicker. He captained Swinton through the war years, during which he represented the Lancashire League, and, in 1919/20, he won 2 caps for Lancashire (and kicked 3 goals in a win over Yorkshire).

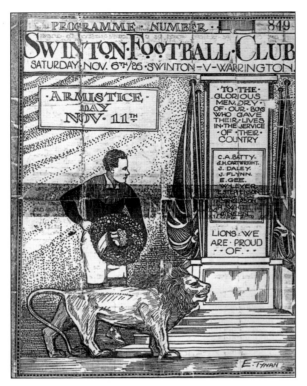

An astonishing thirty-six Swinton players volunteered for armed conflict between 1914 and 1918, and sadly twelve of them did not return. The names of C.A. Batty, J.H. Cartwright, George Crabtree, Jack Daley, Jack Flynn, Ezra Gee, Bill Lever, Tom Neen, Albert Sanderson, Herbert Shedlock, Ernie Stephenson and H. White are listed on this poignant memorial. The best known of these was Flynn, who came to Swinton from Parton in 1904. He won 6 caps for Cumberland, then had a spell with Broughton Rangers before returning to the Lions in 1911. The roll of honour depicted here has been taken from a 1926 programme cover.

A Swinton 'silk', *c*. 1920. These items appeared in packets of BDV Cigarettes and were eagerly collected by schoolboys of the day.

Yours Truly.
T. McCormick.

Tom McCormick and Jimmy Arnold, a forward and a half-back respectively, were never the most revered of Lions during the early 1920s, but they offered strength in depth following the vital rebuilding which took place after the war.

With the club financially crippled following the war, the Lions' directors made a bold decision to gamble 'all or nothing'. In the summer of 1920, local businessmen, particularly Sir Lees Knowles, a wealthy land and colliery owner (who was appointed club president in return), were encouraged to invest capital. The cash raised was spent on ground improvements and the recruitment of exciting new talent. It was hoped that the Swinton public would respond to this initiative, otherwise the club might be doomed. Thankfully, it paid off, helped in no small part by the arrival of arguably the Lions' most influential signings of all time – Albert Jenkins (right) and Hector Halsall (left). Jenkins was a sensational half-back from Ebbw Vale, whose lightning feet and trickery with the ball revolutionised Swinton's attacking play. Halsall arrived almost by accident from Wigan but, from 1922/23, he was appointed captain and went on to provide inspirational leadership to Swinton for the remainder of the 1920s.

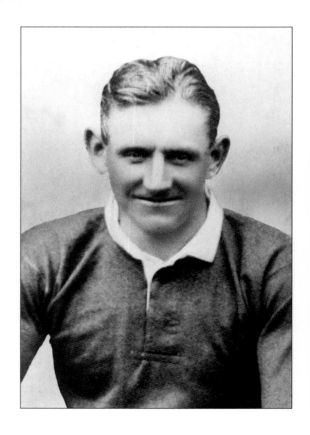

In the close season of 1921, Swinton raided Llanelly to add the flying Welsh international winger, Frank Evans, to their playing staff. Evans had electric speed and an extraordinary side-step, talents which would bring him an all-time club record number of tries (197) under Rugby League rules by the time he retired in 1930. In 1924, he became Swinton's first Rugby League tourist, and when he played in the second test at Sydney, he became the first Swinton player to gain a full test cap. He won 3 further caps during the tour, scoring a total of 3 tries. Pictured here in Welsh colours, he also won 7 caps for the Principality, notching 7 tries in the process.

On 16 November 1921, under the captaincy of Jimmy Dawson, Swinton defeated the Australians for the first time. A try by Frank Evans and three Billy Britton goals gave the Lions a 9-0 success, and marked the only occasion during this particular tour that Australia failed to score a point.

R.L. C.p. semi final 1923.

No. 18   APRIL 21st, 1923.   PRICE 2d.

✠✠ H. C. & A. C. ✠✠
Official Programme

HUDDERSFIELD
v
SWINTON

FRED WOOD | *for* **Quality**
The Hatter | **and Value**

Lion Buildings | All the Latest Styles in Gent's, Hats, Caps & and Hosiery &

Directly Opposite TRAMWAY OFFICES

:: HUDDERSFIELD :: | TELEPHONE——1777

FOOTBALL SHIRTS

The H. C. & A. C. SHIRTS have stood the Test for years. HARD WEAR AND :: PERFECTLY FAST COLOURS ::

Supplied by—
W. H. DAWSON & SONS
Gent's Outfitters, 22 NEW ST., HUDDERSFIELD

OWEN & SON, Printers, etc., 29 Queen St., Huddersfield.

In season 1922/23, the rejuvinated Lions finished third in the newly titled Rugby League and contested the Championship semi-final at Fartown against Huddersfield.

The four prominent Swinton players attempting to cover the Huddersfield winger in the afore-mentioned match (from left to right) are Jack Evans, Hector Halsall, Miller Strong and Frank Evans. Swinton eventually lost 16-5, but hopes remained high for this emerging young Swinton team.

Improvements to the Chorley Road enclosure, which at its height boasted a capacity of around 25,000, ensured that county football returned to Swinton in November 1922. Lancashire won this game comfortably, 46-9. In all, Chorley Road was utilised for county fixtures on five occasions between 1894 and 1928, the first two of which were under Rugby Union rules.

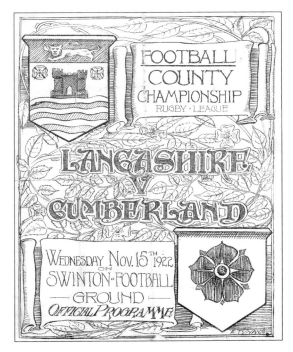

Swinton line up at the start of 1924/25. From left to right, back row: Harry Entwistle, Fred Beswick, Bert Morris, Miller Strong, Henry Blewer, Tom Halliwell, Billy Price, Frank Evans. Front row: Jack Evans, Chris Brockbank, Hector Halsall (captain), Billo Rees, Albert Atkinson. At the end of this campaign, the Lions reached the Championship final for the first time. However, they were unlucky to be defeated 9-5 by Hull Kingston Rovers in a controversial match at Rochdale. The capture of the Lancashire League for the first time offered consolation.

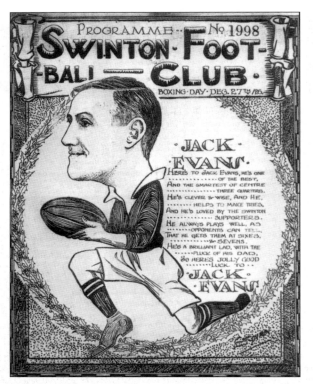

If Halsall provided the leadership and Jenkins the inspiration, then the brains undoubtedly belonged to Jack Evans. The son of his namesake, he signed for the Lions from Swinton Park in 1919 at the age of twenty-two. Evans was a truly gifted centre, and he played a pivotal role in Swinton's successes of the mid-to-late 1920s. His proudest moment came when he skippered the Lions to a Challenge Cup final victory over Oldham in 1926. He was capped 3 times by Great Britain, 7 times by England and 11 times by Lancashire. He toured Australasia in 1928, but made only 3 appearances before being struck down by appendicitis. During the First World War, he had been held prisoner for eight months and he also suffered a gas attack. All these factors led to ill-health, and he was to die at the age of just forty-two.

Having lost the Lancashire Cup final to St Helens Recreation two years previously, the Lions at last claimed the trophy for the first time in December 1925. Wigan were defeated 15-11 at The Cliff, Broughton, and ten of the players involved were, from left to right: Billo Rees, Bert Morris, Chris Brockbank, Harry Entwistle, Fred Beswick, Frank Evans, Henry Blewer, Miller Strong, Jack Evans and Tom Halliwell. Missing are Jack Pearson, Hector Halsall and Bryn Evans.

A very rare shot of the Chorley Road ground, as Swinton take to the field against St Helens Recreation on 6 September 1924. The Lions emerging from the tunnel are Hector Halsall, Bob Williams, Bryn Evans and Jack Evans. On Good Friday 1925, the ground saw its record attendance of 22,000 for the visit of Oldham.

The Critic. OFFICIAL PROGRAMME,
Price 2d.

ROCHDALE HORNETS FOOTBALL CLUB.
SEASON 1925-6.

Rugby League Challenge Cup.

FINAL TIE.

OLDHAM v. SWINTON

AT THE
ATHLETIC GROUNDS, ROCHDALE,
MAY 1st, 1926.   Kick-off 3-30.

CALL
AT THE JUNCTION HOTEL.
OLDHAM ROAD,

10 minutes from
Grounds.
5 minutes from Station.

JOE BOWERS,
The Old
ROCHDALE
HORNETS,
AND
LANCASHIRE
COUNTY
PLAYER,
AND
NORTHERN
UNION TOURIST.

A Welcome to Old
and New Friends.

Large and Small
Parties Catered for.

Phone Rochdale 1261.

By defeating Batley, Broughton
Rangers, Hull Kingston Rovers
and Halifax in 1926, the Lions
reached their first Challenge Cup
final for twenty-six years. With
Halsall out injured, Jack Evans
skippered the team to a 9-3 victory
over Oldham in front of a 27,000
crowd at the Athletic Grounds,
Rochdale. Oldham would get their
revenge against an injury-ravaged
Lions in the 1927 final.

Halsall's place in the 1926 cup final team went to Wilf Sulway, who had been signed from the Welsh RU side Talywain in 1924. Sulway went on to have a fine game, and he also provided valuable cover in 1928 when he also played in the Championship final, during which he set up the opening try for Hector Halsall.

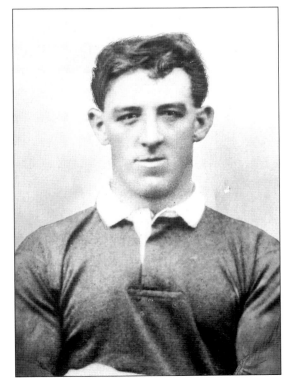

The decisive try of the 1926 Challenge Cup final was, by all accounts, a bizarre effort scored by the Swinton hooker, Henry Blewer. In all, local lad Blewer would win three Championships, two Challenge Cups and two Lancashire Cups with Swinton, in a career spanning a colossal 445 appearances between 1919 and 1931.

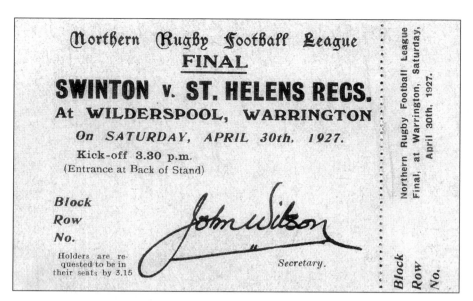

Northern Rugby Football League
Final, at Warrington, Saturday,
April 30th, 1927.

Northern Rugby Football League
FINAL

SWINTON v. ST. HELENS RECS.

At WILDERSPOOL, WARRINGTON

On SATURDAY, APRIL 30th, 1927.

Kick-off 3.30 p.m.
(Entrance at Back of Stand)

Block

Row

No.

John Wilson

Secretary.

Holders are requested to be in their seats by 3.15

Block Row No.

Swinton's rise to the fore was confirmed when, in 1926/27, they landed their first Championship. After ruthlessly putting Wigan to the sword by a score of 23-3 in the semi-final at Chorley Road, the Lions met St Helens Recreation in the final at Wilderspool, Warrington. They won 13-8 with two sensational individual tries by Bryn Evans and another by Fred Beswick. Prop-forward Bert Morris, a capture from Coventry RUFC, kicked two goals.

This is the squad which not only won the 1927 Championship, but went on to defend it in spectacular style. From left to right, back row: H. Edwards, George Norrey, Jack Robertson, Billy Wallwork, R. Crowshaw, Tom Crossley (all directors), Sam Jones (secretary), Tommy Mee (assistant trainer). Middle row: J. Mee (attendant), Dick Cracknell, Harry Entwistle, Bert Morris, Henry Blewer, Miller Strong, Wilf Sulway, Fred Beswick, Elwyn Leigh, Billy Kearns (trainer). Front row: Jack Scholes (director), Frank Evans, Jack Pearson, Jack Evans, Hector Halsall (captain), Chris Brockbank, Bryn Evans, Sir Lees Knowles (president), Ted Worsley (chairman). Cross-legged, Albert Atkinson and Billo Rees.

The ultimate goal in Rugby League, until the abolition of the County Leagues in 1970, was to win 'All Four Cups'. The Hunslet and Huddersfield teams of 1908 and 1915 achieved such immortality, and they were to be joined in 1928 by Swinton – the last club to achieve this incredible distinction. The pride of having won their first Championship is evident from this illustration taken from the programme cover for the opening game of season 1927/28.

A key figure of the Lions' great teams of the 1920s and 1930s was Bryn Evans, the younger brother of Jack. He joined the Lions from Swinton Park in 1920, and soon made his mark as an elusive and intelligent stand-off. He first enjoyed success playing alongside Albert Jenkins, and then later with Billo Rees, with whom he created the most effective half-back partnership of his era. As the caption indicates, it took a while before he earned his first cap in 1927 but, between then and 1933, he gained 10 test caps. Twice, in 1928 and 1932, he toured Australia with Great Britain, and he also appeared 4 times for England and 21 times for Lancashire. With 468 appearances to his name, only Ken Gowers, Jim Valentine and Martin Hodgson played more games for Swinton. Evans was a modest and unassuming man who enjoyed the utmost respect in the Rugby League world. He died in July 1975 at the age of seventy-five.

The other cog in the Lions' sensational half-back partnership was Billo Rees. Rees was a Welsh international trialist who was signed from Llanelly in 1921. After finally dislodging Albert Jenkins from the team, he developed into a scrum-half of rare talent. He possessed great speed from a standing start, and was a master of the clever grubber-kick. Between 1926 and 1930, he won 11 caps for Great Britain (scoring 2 tries), as well as gaining 6 caps for Wales.

The first of the five trophies won by the Lions in 1927/28 was the Lancashire Cup and, for the second time in three years, it was Wigan who were beaten in the final. Before a 22,000 crowd at Watersheddings, Oldham, Swinton raced into a 5-0 lead with a try from Fred Beswick and a conversion from Bert Morris. After half-time, Wigan hit back with a Jim Sullivan penalty, then, in the last minute, Swinton winger Frank Evans was forced to make a miraculous last-ditch tackle to preserve a final result of 5-2.

Swinton-born Chris Brockbank made his Lions' debut as a sixteen-year-old during the First World War. He went on to form an excellent wing-centre partnership with Hector Halsall and was a scorer of many vital tries. Indeed, with 142 efforts, he is the Lions' sixth top try-scorer of all-time. He was twice Swinton's top try-scorer and, on 6 April 1927, he gained an England cap when Wales were defeated at Broughton. After his playing days ended, he became secretary at Warrington and, in 1954, was hugely responsible for helping to set up the new Blackpool Borough club.

14 April 1928. The last time that the Challenge Cup was held in Swinton arms. Victorious skipper Hector Halsall clutches the coveted trophy as he is chaired off the Central Park pitch by jubilant Swinton supporters.

Dine at the . . .

MINORCA
GRILL ROOM

Wallgate, Wigan.

(Nearly opposite Station).

Chops and Steaks from the Grill.

LUNCHEONS,

AFTERNOON TEAS,

GARAGE.

Tel. 353.

S. T. CROOK

LADIES' GENTS' CHILDREN'S

HAIRDRESSING

in every Branch.

ALL TOILET REQUISITES
IN STOCK.

5, LIBRARY ST., WIGAN.

Tel.: Wigan 1126.

For
SMART EYEWEAR
at Reasonable Charges
Consult
CYRIL KERSHAW, F.B.O.A.
50, MARKET ST., WIGAN.

"Sunday Pictorial"
£10,000 Football Contest

Order YOUR Copy To-day.

SWINTON. 5   3—WARRINGTON.

		Height ft. in.	Weight st. lb.			Height ft. ins.	Weight st. lb.
	Full Back:				**Full Back:**		
1.	W. YOUNG	5 6	11 8	1. A. FROWEN	5 8½	10 11
	Three-Quarters:				**Three-Quarters:**		
2.	F. EVANS	5 6	10 6	2. W. H. RHODES	5 9½	12 0
3.	H. HALLSALL	5 6	11 9	3. J. O. MEREDITH	6 1	13 10
4.	J. EVANS	5 8	11 7	4. L. PERKINS	5 10	14 4
5.	C. BROCKBANK	5 6	11 2	5. D. M. DAVIES	5 7	11 0
	Half-Backs:				**Half-Backs:**		
6.	B. EVANS	5 6	10 10	6. T. FLYNN	5 8	11 6
7.	W. REES	5 4	10 7	7. W. KIRK	5 8	11 4
	Forwards:				**Forwards:**		
8.	M. F. STRONG	5 10	13 7	8. W. CUNLIFFE	5 10½	14 10
9.	H. BLEWER	5 10	13 0	9. A. PEACOCK	5 10	13 4
10.	H. E. MORRIS	5 9	13 0	10. J. MILLER	5 8	14 3
11.	M. HODGSON	5 11	13 0	11. F. WILLIAMS	5 10	14 2
12.	R. H. CRACKNELL	6 0		12. TRANTER	6 0	13 6
13.	F. BESWICK	5 8	12 0	13. C. SEELING	5 10	12 6

Referee: Mr. H. Horsfall (Batley).

Touch Judges: Mr. J. Thomas (Wigan) and Mr. J. Houghton (St. Helens).

RE-ARRANGED MATCHES.

Wednesday, April 18th—WIGAN v. WARRINGTON. Kick-off 5-45 p.m.
Saturday, April 21st—WIGAN v. HULL. Kick-off 3-30 p.m.
Wednesday, April 25th—WIGAN "A" v. OLDHAM "A". Kick-off 6-15 p.m.
Saturday, April 28th—WIGAN v. DEWSBURY. Kick-off 3-30 p.m.

As the Lancashire Senior Competition match Wigan "A" v. Oldham "A" on Wednesday, April 25th, will practically settle the "A" Team Championship a good game can be expected.

The prize for the lucky number will be 5/-, not 10/- as stated on back page.
Last Prizewinner, April 6th—Mr. H. Critchley, 194, Windleshaw Road, St. Helens.

Messrs. JOHN SUMNER & Co.,

LIMITED.

Haigh Brewery, Wigan,

EXHIBITED BREWERS' EXHIBITION 1919-20-21-25-26.

Awarded:—

THREE FIRSTS.   FIVE SECONDS.   ONE THIRD.

SUPPORT LOCAL ALES.

Tel.: 250.

Scott & Worthin

CHEMISTS AND
PHOTOGRAPHIC DEALE

6, MARKET ST., WIG

Tel.: 265.

"Wolstencroft

T Clothiers,
H Hatters, and
E General Outfitters.

5, 7 & 9, Cowling Buildi
Mesnes, Street, WIGAN

The Best that is Bott

YOUR HEALTH!

Combe's London Stout

Agents and Bottlers:—

"THE BOTTLERS,"

E. Dickinson & C

101, Darlington St. East, W
Telephone

E. SIDEBOTHAM, 31, MILLGATE, WIGAN.   PRINTING BY THE LATEST LABOUR-SAVING METHODS.

With the Lancashire League Championship safely secured, the Lions attempted to win their third trophy when they reached the Challenge Cup final, thanks to victories over Whitehaven Recreation, Halifax, Castleford and Hull. Swinton's opponents at Central Park, Wigan (the last final before the Wembley era) were Warrington, for which a 33,909 crowd had gathered. A Chris Brockbank try was cancelled out by a Warrington equaliser but, towards the end of the match, the cup was won courtesy of a dramatic Jack Evans drop-goal.

Buy a "TELEMAC"
FROM
Longworths
AND WATCH
THE MATCH IN COMFORT
PRICES:—
21/- & **29/6**
GUARANTEED FOR
— 2 YEARS —

ALEXANDER
THOMSON
Telephone 463 & 465 & Cen.
LETTERPRESS PRINTER
LITHOGRAPHERS.
ACCOUNT BOOK MAKER
WAREHOUSE   WORKS
8 PRINCESS | BOARDMAN
ST   ST
MANCHESTER | MILES PLATTING
PRINTER OF THIS PROGRAMME

If you want a
square deal in
Furniture
THEN CONSULT.
HAROLD
MORRIS
HOUSE FURNISHER
9. CHORLEY RD
SWINTON
Telephone Eccles 231

For Tasty
Bits
H.K.MASON
109B MANCHESTER
— ROAD —
SWINTON

ECCLES
1108 / ECCLES
1108
HEYS
LION GARAGE
CORNER OF WORSLEY RD.
CLOSED & OPEN CARS
— FOR HIRE —
WEDDINGS OUR SPECIALITY
COMFORT & SATISFACTION ASSURED
YOUR PLEASURE IS
OUR BUISNESS

SATURDAY APRIL 28TH /28
SWINTON
V
HUNSLET
KICK OFF 3.30 P.M.
PERIOD OF PLAY 40 mins EACH WAY
SWINTON · HUNSLET.

	SWINTON	HUNSLET	
1	W. YOUNG.	J. PLACE	1
2	F. EVANS.	G BROUGHTON	2
3	H. HALSALL	J. NICHOLSON	3
4	E. LEIGH.	J. WALKINGTON	4
5	C. BROCKBANK	J. COULSON.	5
6	A. ATKINSON	E. YOUNG	6
7	H. EVANS.	W. THORNTON	7
8	M. E. STRONG	C. LITT.	8
9	H. BLEWER	L. WHITE.	9
10	H. MORRIS.	J. TRAILL.	10
11	M. HODGSON.	H. MOSS.	11
12	R. H. CRACKNELL	H. CROWTHER	12
13	F. BESWICK.	J. W. GUERIN	13
14	W. SULWAY.	G CHAPMAN.	14
15		D. JENKINS	15

REFEREE M. F. PEEL.
Touchjudge (Red) . J. GERRARD
"   " (White) . J. LOFTUS.

This programme may be worth 3/- or
2/- to you. Look out for board at
Half Time and if winner apply to
Programme Manager after the match.

FLATULENCE
— TABLETS —
WIND & INDIGESTION
YATES BROS
Chemists. **1/-**

JOHN·G·PERCY
A RELIABLE TOBACCONIST
6. STATION RD
SWINTON
EVERYTHING
— FOR —
SMOKERS

YOU CAN STAND THE ILLS
& ENJOY THE THRILL
IF YOUR BOOTS
are repaired at
HANKINSONS
The Leading Dept Repair-
ers, Leather & Grindery Dealers
3. STATION·RD
III, WORSLEY·RD.
· SWINTON ·
over 50 years experience

·G·H·
McLACLAN
BUTCHER
131, PARTINGTON
LANE
SWINTON

CALL & HAVE A
PLEASANT HOUR
BEFORE &
AFTER
RED LION
THE
MATCH
AT THE
HOTEL
308 SPRUCE PROPRIETOR
S.R.F.C
CONCERTS, FRID, SAT & MON,
7.30 to 10.30

FULLY JEWELLED
MOVEMENT
THE·LIONLEVER 15/6
GUARANTEED FOR 5 YEARS.
LION LEVER
H·COLLIER & SON
JEWELLERS, 105 & 143. CHORLEY ROAD.
SWINTON

Sight Testing
BY
H.V. COLLIER
F.B.O.A. F.I.O. (LOND).
OPTHALMIC·OPTICIAN
143, CHORLEY ROAD
NEAR·SWINTON CAR·TERMINUS.

With Bryn Evans, Jack Evans and Billo Rees en route to Australia, Swinton would have to win the Championship the hard way. With arguably their three most influential players out of the team, they first of all had to overcome Hunslet in a Chorley Road semi-final. Albert Atkinson came in at stand-off, and Harold 'Chick' Evans replaced his older brother, Bryn, at scrum-half. Billy Young and Elwyn Leigh also made rare appearances, but even with this unfamiliar line-up, progress to the final was achieved with a 12-2 victory.

Relative newcomers to Rugby League, Featherstone Rovers, were the Lions' opponents in the 1928 Championship final, but they proved no match for the rampant Lions. Tries from Hector Halsall, Frank Evans and Dick Cracknell, and a late goal by Billy Young, gave Swinton a very comfortable 11-0 victory. 'All Four Cups' belonged to Swinton, and, indeed, a fifth was added when Broughton Rangers were defeated in the final of the Salford Royal Hospital Cup in front of a Chorley Road crowd numbering some 9,000.

The zenith in the history of a proud rugby club – the glorious five cups team of 1927/28. From left to right, back row: Tommy Mee (assistant trainer), Dr E. Higson, Tom Crossley, Jack Robertson, George Norrey, Billy Wallwork (all directors). Third Row: Sam Jones (secretary), Alf Pardon, Frank Buckingham, Jack Fairhurst, Miller Strong, Jack Pearson, Elwyn Leigh, Wilf Sulway, J. Mee (attendant). Second row: Billy Kerns (trainer), Fred Beswick, Harry Entwisle, Tom Halliwell, Fred Butters, Martin Hodgson, Dick Cracknell, Albert Grimshaw, Bert Morris, Billy Young. Front row: Ted Worsley (chairman), Harold Evans, Chris Brockbank, Jack Evans, Hector Halsall (captain), Bryn evans, Frank Evans, Jack Scholes (director). Seated on floor: Albert Atkinson, Billo Rees.

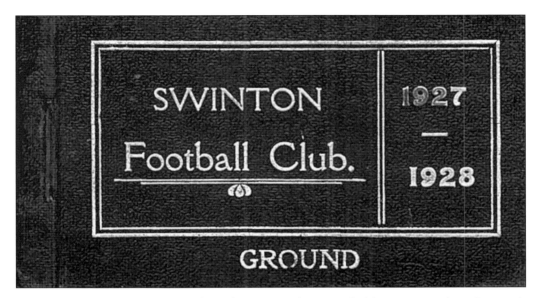

Season 1927/28 would certainly have been a good year to hold a season ticket. Swinton's achievements have been painstakingly detailed in fountain pen on the inside covers by the former owner of this unique piece of Swinton memorabilia.

Out in Australasia, Billo Rees was carving an enviable reputation for himself, and when Britain faced Central Queensland, he was proud to accept the captaincy of the team as characterised here. During the tour, he played in all 6 test matches and appeared in a further 13 tour matches, scoring 3 tries. Both Australia and New Zealand were defeated 2-1.

In 1928, a long-running dispute with the landowner of the Chorley Road ground, Thomas 'Totty' White, came to a head. Refusing to be held ransom to their own success, the Lions reluctantly decided to vacate Chorley Road and build a new ground next to the railway line off Station Road, on land purchased for £2,000. The construction lasted approximately twelve months, and shown here is an excavating machine loading up jubilee wagons as work progressed to level the site of the playing field. It was estimated that the total process would cost £6,000, but the final sum came to £11,000. Ironically, Totty White had wanted just £9,000 for the Chorley Road freehold.

On 2 March 1929, the first match was staged at Station Road. A crowd of 22,000 saw Swinton defeat Wigan by 9 points to 3. However, it ultimately turned out to be a frustrating season for the Lions, and only the Lancashire League trophy was retained.

The ground was opened by Sir Edwin Stockton MP, who declared: 'I congratulate the directors on making this magnificent ground and I think you are going to have one of the best grounds in the country. It is what Swinton deserve. Swinton have always gone by the name of the Lions and they deserve such a name as last season they achieved what no other rugby club has ever done. We have a great crowd today, and I hope that Swinton will win, but if they do not I know that the game will be played in the right spirit. I have the greatest pleasure in declaring the ground open for play!'.

Sir EDWIN F. STOCKTON, J.P.

*who will Officially Open
the New Ground*

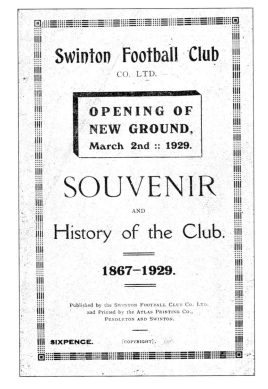

Swinton Football Club
CO. LTD.

OPENING OF
NEW GROUND,
March 2nd :: 1929.

SOUVENIR

AND

History of the Club.

1867–1929.

Published by the SWINTON FOOTBALL CLUB Co. LTD.
and Printed by the ATLAS PRINTING CO.,
PENDLETON AND SWINTON.

SIXPENCE.   [COPYRIGHT].

This superb sixty-page booklet, containing a history of the club to date, was specially commissioned to mark the occasion.

The honour of scoring the Lions' first try on the ground fell to winger Frank Buckingham who, having signed from New Zealand club Waikato RUFC in 1927 (despite having been born in Birmingham), is widely recognised as being the Lions' first overseas signing. Leading 4-3 with two minutes to go, Buckingham jinked in for a try, and when Martin Hodgson added his third goal of the afternoon, it completed a truly memorable day for the club.

Local lad Fred Butters made his first-team debut in 1922/23, but it took a while before he was able to regularly hold down the loose-forward role. He began to blossom fully during the 1928/29 campaign, when he played 3 times for Lancashire, before making his Great Britain test debut at the same time as Martin Hodgson, when Britain levelled the series at Leeds in December 1929. Both retained their places for the decider when Station Road hosted its first international on 4 January 1930, a game which also saw Hector Halsall win his only test cap. It was this game that earned Butters hero status, because with the match deadlocked at 0-0 with seconds to go, Butters tackled the Australian winger, 'Chimpy' Busch, into the corner flag to save the Ashes. He almost ripped his ear off in the process, but Britain went on to win a hastily-arranged fourth test at Rochdale. During their tour, the Australians also went down 9-5 against Swinton.

SALTER & SALTER'S SHOES ARE BEST FOR STYLE, COMFORT AND VALUE

Dine at the

MINORCA GRILL ROOM

Wallgate, Wigan.

(Nearly opposite Station).

Chops and Steaks from the Grill.

LUNCHEONS.

AFTERNOON TEAS.

GARAGE.

Tel. 353.

S. T. CROOK

LADIES', GENTS', CHILDREN'S
HAIRDRESSING
in every Branch.

ALL TOILET REQUISITES
IN STOCK.

5, Library Street, WIGAN.
Tel.: Wigan 1126.

PHILLIP'S

For Eyewear.

QUALIFIED OPTOLOGISTS.

The Sight-Testing Rooms.

48, WALLGATE, and
25, STANDISHGATE,
WIGAN.

WATCH THE MATCH IN COMFORT—WEAR

ALSTEAD'S Overcoats

MADE TO YOUR MEASURE.

Overcoatings made on Alstead's
Wigan Looms by Wigan Workers

ALSTEADS FOR QUALITY

Tel.: 250.

Scott & Worthington

CHEMISTS AND
PHOTOGRAPHIC DEALERS,

6, MARKET ST., WIGAN.

Tel. 210 Leigh.

WILD'S "Big Ben" Scouring Brands.

The only Real Scouring Brand.

THEY DO NOT INJURE
THE HANDS,

HINDLEY GREEN, nr. Wigan.

LEEDS			SWINTON		
Full-back	1	BROUGH	Full-back	1	SCOTT
Three-Qrs.	2	HARRIS	Three-Qrs.	2	BUCKINGHAM
	3	MOORES		3	WHITTAKER
	4	O'ROURKE		4	H. EVANS
	5	SMITH, S.		5	KENNY
Half-Backs	6	WILLIAMS			SULWAY
	7	ADAMS	Half-Backs	6	B. EVANS
Forwards	9	DEMAINE		7	REES
	8	THOMPSON	Forwards	8	WRIGHT
	10	THOMAS		9	BLEWER
	12	SMITH, R.		10	MORRIS
	11	DOUGLAS		11	HODGSON
	13	GILL		12	BESWICK
		JENKINS		13	BUTTERS
		COX			STRONG
		GOULTHORPE			
		GRAINGE			

Referee: Mr. F. Peel (Bradford).
Touch Judges: Mr. J. W. Andrews (Oldham) and Mr. T. Hesketh (Wigan).
Schoolboys' Match—ROSE BRIDGE (Black and Red) v. WHELLEY.

THE "GOAL" OF ALL BEER DRINKERS
IS TO GET THE BEST—

Call at any of Haigh Brewery Houses and "TRY" Ours.

John Sumner & Co. Limited, Haigh Brewery

The Best that is Bottled.

YOUR HEALTH!

COOMBE'S LONDON STOUT.
IS KNOWN EVERYWHERE

Agents and Bottlers:—

"THE BOTTLERS,"

E. Dickinson & Co.,

101, Darlington St. East, Wigan.
Telephone 599.

E. SIDEBOTHAM, 31, MILLGATE, WIGAN. PRINTING BY THE LATEST LABOUR-SAVING METHODS.

Swinton reached the Championship final again in 1931, where they duly prevented Leeds from landing their first Rugby League title. The Lions won 14-7, thanks to tries from Fred Butters and George Whittaker, with four goals by Martin Hodgson.

Number five Jack Kenny, a Pendlebury lad signed from Leigh to replace Frank Evans, halts a Leeds raid during the 1931 Championship final, as Harold and Bryn Evans rush to lend support. The game took place at Wigan's Central Park and attracted a crowd of 31,000.

Season 1931/32 brought double cup disappointment to the Lions. In the Lancashire Cup, the Lions were defeated 10-8 by Salford at The Cliff, Broughton. The Lions had been rocked by suspensions to Billo Rees and Harold Evans, leaving rookies Johnny Jones and Hughie Salmon to fill their rather large boots. The match ended in controversy and heartbreak for Salmon. With the scores locked at 8-8, the youngster was penalised for apparently delaying a play-the-ball, and Salford landed a winning penalty with the last kick of the game. Here the game is depicted by Gannon of the *Daily Dispatch*.

54

The Lions also reached the Challenge Cup final, following a semi-final victory over Wakefield Trinity. With a tour of Australasia impending, it was decided to bring cup final day forward. However, this meant that Wembley was double-booked, and the RFL reluctantly brought the final back north to Central Park. Swinton would never reach another final, and, therefore, would never play beneath the famous Twin Towers. This particular game was also lost: 11-8 to Leeds. Martin Hodgson kicked four goals, whilst Leeds' decisive try was the only one Swinton conceded throughout their entire cup campaign. Here, Bryn Evans passes out to Fred Butters.

More action from the 1932 Challenge Cup final. Bryn Evans looks for an opening, as Fred Butters pulls away from the scrum. Billo Rees can be seen between the two Swinton men.

In the summer of 1932, Bryn Evans was selected to tour Austalasia for the second time – on this occasion, as vice-captain to Jim Sullivan. He played in five tests – twice against Australia and three times against New Zealand – and was a winner on each occasion. Evans was awarded a testimonial soon after his return to Swinton.

The 1932 Great Britain squad aboard *SS Jervis Bay*. Bryn Evans is fourth from the right on the middle row, whilst the other Swinton tourists are: Martin Hodgson (standing third from right), Fred Butters (standing second from left) and prop-forward Joe Wright (middle row, far right). Wright played in the final match of the tour against New Zealand at Carlaw Park to earn his only test cap. Sadly, Butters' contribution was reduced to a single minor appearance due to injury.

In 1933, the Lions yet again reached the Championship final but, on this occasion, a bitter struggle was was lost against Salford, 15-5. Fred Butters is the man tackled, whilst the three players to the left of the picture are Billo Rees, Billy Shaw and Fred Beswick. The game took place at Central Park in front of a disappointing crowd of 18,000 – the attendance was affected mainly because both sets of supporters had unsuccessfully campaigned for the match to take place at The Cliff.

THE RUGBY FOOTBALL LEAGUE.

OFFICIAL
Souvenir Programme

THIRD TEST MATCH.

England v. Australia,
ON SWINTON GROUND,
Saturday, December 16th, 1933.
KICK-OFF AT 2-30.

Price - - - TWOPENCE.

ATLAS PRINTING CO., PENDLETON.

In December 1933, Station Road was again the venue for a Test match between Great Britain and Australia. With Martin Hodgson and hooker Tommy Armitt (making his test debut) in the British ranks, a series whitewash was completed with a 19-16 victory. The Australians had also lost 10-4 to Swinton on the ground a few weeks earlier.

Swinton Football Club

CO., LTD.

OFFICIAL		ONE
PROGRAMME.		PENNY.

Season - 1934-35.

WELL CAUGHT SIR!

President: T. SAVILLE WHITTLE, Esq.

Directors:

T. CROSSLEY, Esq.	G. NORREY, Esq.
H. EDWARDS, Esq.	J. C. ROBERTSON, Esq.
DR. E. HIGSON.	W. WALLWORK, Esq.
D. P. LEES, Esq.	H. S. WARBURTON, Esq.

E. W. WORSLEY, Esq., J.P.,
(Rugby League Council and Lancashire County Representative).

Secretary: S. JONES.
Registered Office: 66, Station Road, Swinton, near Manchester.

By 1934/35, the Lions were building another great team. If the side of the late 1920s was built around the attacking flair of the brothers Evans, together with Welshmen Billo Rees and Frank Evans, then this new Swinton team was built on awesome forward power. Cumbrians Joe Wright and Martin Hodgson, together with Tommy Armitt and Fred Butters, were all proud holders of test caps. Welsh prop-forward Gomer Hughes was an established international forward under both codes, whilst there was also the great experience of Fred Beswick. This programme cover is from the Lions' fourth Championship-winning season in eight years.

By beating Salford 10-2 in front of a Station Road crowd of 20,202 in the last four play-off, the Lions booked their place in the Championship final against Warrington. The match took place at Central Park, Wigan, where Swinton were victorious (14-3) in front of a 27,700 crowd. For Bryn Evans, it was the second time he had lifted the trophy. It was a proud moment when he told the crowd, 'Thank you for the way you have supported us. All the team played for Swinton and not for themselves. To captain such a great team is easy.'

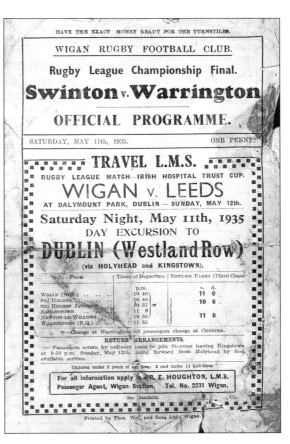

The Championship victory also marked the last game in the eventful career of the Lions' loose-forward, Fred Beswick. He had made his Swinton debut in September 1924, and his career had spanned five championship finals, four Challenge Cup finals and three Lancashire Cup finals. Beswick was a ferocious tackler and the scorer of important tries: attributes which brought him 5 caps for Lancashire. As a native of Warrington, it was fitting that his finest hour in a Swinton jersey should come against his home-town team. At the final whistle, the crowd chanted 'We want Beswick!' and they then carried their hero from the pitch shoulder high in emotional scenes. In later life, he became a director at Warrington, yet would always wear a Swinton badge on his blazer.

As champions of the Rugby League, the Lions were invited to tour France in May 1935. They played a total of 4 matches and were winners on each occasion. French champions Villeneuve were beaten 27-25, then came Pau (19-8), Cognac (29-22), and a South West Select at Nantes (29-22). The programme cover depicted is that from the final game.

60

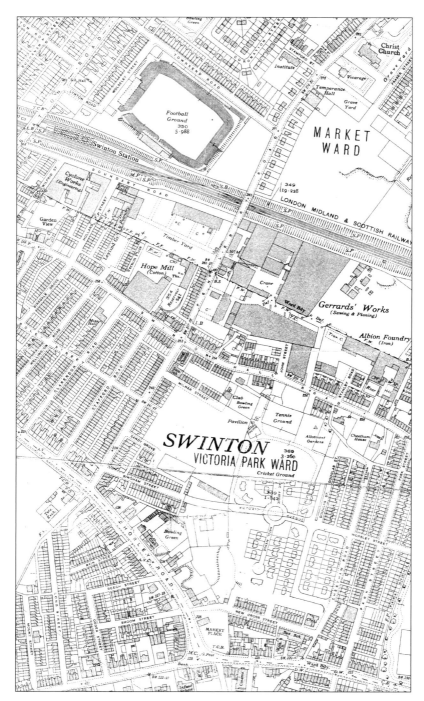

The Ordnance Survey map of 1936 clearly shows the Station Road ground in its prime. The layout of the ground would remain unaltered for another forty years or so. The new housing between Hazel Avenue and Cheetham Road (towards the bottom of the map) indicates the precise position of the former Chorley Road ground. The old Swinton Cricket ground is also in the process of being built over.

By 1936, the Lions' legendary second-rower, Martin Hodgson, had reached his prime. Signed from Egremont RUFC in 1927 at the age of seventeen, he was now the proud owner of three Championship winners medals. He toured Down Under in 1932, but it was on his second tour of 1936 that he struck fear into his Australian opponents and gained the reputation of being the finest cover-tackler the game had ever seen. The Second World War would curtail his career, but even so, by then he had amassed 477 appearances (surpassed only by Ken Gowers and Jim Valentine) and 875 goals. He was also Swinton's most capped player with 16, on top of which he gained 9 caps for England and 29 for Cumberland.

Hooker Tommy Armitt accompanied Hodgson on the 1936 tour and, between 1933 and 1937, he won 8 test caps. Signed from a local junior club in 1930, he made his debut at the opening of Barrow's Craven Park in August 1931. Again, the war disrupted his career, during which he refused a testimonial because he felt that the club could ill-afford it. Armitt played on briefly until October 1946, and there can be little doubt that he was Swinton's finest ever hooker.

Great Britain's 13-3 victory over Australia on 13 November 1937 was the third time a Test Match had been staged at Station Road. The picture shows the old scoreboard in the background, as well as part of the 31,724 crowd. Swinton fans had threatened a boycott at the exclusion of Martin Hodgson, but they had the consolation of seeing a Man of the Match performance by Tommy Armitt. Eleven days later, a Fred Butters try and a Hodgson goal gave Swinton a 5-3 victory (their fourth in a row) over the Aussies.

After a couple of indifferent seasons, the Lions looked set to return to winning trophies in 1937/38. This action shot is from the Salford v. Swinton derby at The Willows on 16 April 1938, which the Lions lost 9-5. The men making the tackle are Jack Stoddart (left) and Gomer Hughes. Joe Wright is stood in the backdrop.

Here's Hoping For . . . . . A First Class Game

Well, this is the Semi-Final! It's rather a pity that these two teams should meet. How much better it would have been had both been going to Wembley to settle their little difference at the mecca of all good football fans.

Of course, both teams are confident! Isn't that the usual thing before all great games? And this should be a great game.

To go on to the Final and win is, of course, my Team's ambition. That is something we have never done. Our opponents are one-up on us there, because they have

Says
Lance B. Todd
Secretary-Manager
Salford R.F.C.

already done the trick—but not at Wembley. They reached the Final in 1932, but unfortunately, owing to the fact that a touring side was going abroad, the Final was played in the North—which, of course, was mighty hard luck on them.

Anyway — whatever happens to-day, this district will be well represented in London, and if it is not to be Salford, then I can assure Swinton that we will all wish them the best of luck when they trot out on the field down there.

4

Yes, Mr. Todd, it is a pity in a way that we have to meet in the semi-final. What a sensational match a Salford v. Swinton clash would be at Wembley.

Still it is certain to be a grand encounter to-day and while we would naturally be delighted to be journeying to London in May if we win, we shall just as sincerely offer our congratulations to Salford if they make the grade.

We are fielding a strong side and every single player is imbued with Cup Final spirit. I have not the slightest doubt that Salford players are equally confident of victory. That is as it should be.

For years we have been the friendliest yet deadliest rivals, yet it is 38 years since we clashed in a Cup Tie. On that occasion we came out victorious, and I am hoping that history will be re-

Says
Sam Jones
Secretary
Swinton R.F.C.

peated and that we shall make trip to Wembley—for the time, incidentally, though we been Cup winners on three sions and runners-up in two finals.

In that time we have had exciting and close games with Salford friends, and whatever result we have never once cause to complain their play or sportsmanship.

know that to-day same spirit will evident and that ever gains the honour of into the biggest Rugby ever the year will well have des the privilege. So here's match which I hope will down on the rolls of Rugby tory as one in which fine good sportsmanship, thrills action will give every spectat money's worth.

SCORE BOARD KEY—SATURDAY, APRIL 9th, 1938.

The Half-time Scores of the following Matches will be displayed or Score Board as soon as received.

A—Halifax .... v. B—Barrow ....

C—Wigan............................ v. D—Oldham ....

E—Hunslet........................ v. F—Hull ....

5

Swinton and Salford met again in the semi-final of the Challenge Cup with a place at Wembley at stake, but in a highly controversial match at the Belle Vue Stadium in Manchester, the Lions went down 6-0. The official crowd was returned as 30,000, but neutral observers estimated that as many as 50,000 had forced their way into the enclosure. This resulted in chaotic scenes around the touchlines, which arguably contributed to Salford's decisive try. Here, the two secretaries, Sam Jones and Lance Todd, preview proceedings. Swinton also went down in the Championship semi-final against Leeds.

Swinton winger Jack McGurk in action during a 10-0 victory over Wigan at Station Road in April 1939. A year later, McGurk was the hero of the Lions' Lancashire Cup final victory over Widnes

SWINTON RUGBY FOOTBALL CLUB,

SWINTON, MANCHESTER.

Official Programme.

LANCASHIRE CUP.—FINAL TIE.

Swinton v. Widnes

Saturday, April 27th, 1940,

AT STATION ROAD, SWINTON.   KICK-OFF AT 3-30.

Forthcoming League Fixtures :

Saturday, May 11.—SWINTON v. BARROW, at Barrow.
(KICK-OFF 3-15 P.M.)

Monday, May 13.—SWINTON v. WIGAN, at Wigan (3-30)

SWINTON v. BROUGHTON, at Swinton.
(Date being arranged)

Saturday, May 4th, on the Salford Ground—

REPRESENTATIVE MATCH for RED CROSS

Programme - One Penny.

Atlas Printing Co., Pendleton, Swinton, and Eccles.

It was during the Lancashire Cup semi-final second leg in April 1940 that Martin Hodgson booted a world record 77 ¾ yard penalty against Rochdale Hornets at the Athletic Grounds. Attempts by a Salford historian to undermine this achievement, and apparently accepted without sufficient cross-referencing in certain quarters, show total disrespect to this legend of the Rugby League field. With Randall Lewis (a former Aberavon policeman and record £1,000 signing) and Jack McGurk excelling themselves, a two-legged final against Widnes was not settled until the dying minutes of extra time.

BRADFORD NORTHERN   OFFICIAL PROGRAMME 1d.

RUGBY LEAGUE WAR-TIME CHAMPIONSHIP

Bradford Northern v. Swinton in Odsal Decider.

By the Editor.

OWING to war circumstances, it is necessary for us to cut down to-day's programme drastically. Effort is made, therefore, to tell you as much as possible in the space available.

To-day's meeting of Bradford Northern and Swinton at Odsal is to decide the Rugby League's War-time Championship. Neither medals nor a cup will be presented, but this "grand final" as it has been called in official circles, is for the game's championship.

Swinton are the champions of the Lancashire League; Northern have that honour in Yorkshire. In the first meeting between the teams, Northern won by three goals, five tries (21 points) to two goals, three tries (13 points) at Swinton last Saturday.

Bradford Northern Football Club, Ltd.

President :
SIR HENRY P. PRICE.

Directors :
J. HEPWORTH, Esq., J.P., M.P. (Chairman).
H. HORNBY, Esq. (Vice-Chairman).
E. CRAVEN, Esq.   L. DOBSON, Esq.
R. C. YABLON, Esq., LL.B. (Hon. Solicitor).
T. J. ROBINSON, Esq., J.P.

Hon. Surgeons :
DR. J. WRIGHT, New Cross Street, West Bowling
DR. H. SPARROW, "Lismore," Smith Av., Wibsey
DR. H. FIDLER, 397 Tong Street, Dudley Hill.
H. HORNBY, Esq. (Managing Director).

Team Manager :   Ground :
Mr. DAI REES   Odsal Stadium.
Telephone 7429
Colours : Red, Amber and Black   May 25th, 1940

Having won the Lancashire War League, Swinton faced Bradford Northern over two legs to decide the overall 1940 Championship. Having lost the home leg 21-13, Swinton left themselves a mountain to climb, and, indeed, the second leg was also lost, 16-9.

After living under the shadow of his illustrious older brothers, Harold Evans had gradually emerged during the 1930s as a fine player in his own right. He was signed in 1925 as a seventeen-year-old, but such were the Lions' riches that it took him a while to earn a regular spot. He had the qualities of being solid, reliable and adaptable, but Evans was also good enough to be capped for Lancashire. In May 1939, he was a worthy recipient of a joint testimonial with Fred Butters.

With the onset of the Second World War, Station Road came under the jurisdiction of the Home Guard from the summer of 1940 until July 1943. Therefore, during season 1940/41, the Lions were forced to play their Emergency War League fixtures at The Willows. From 1943 until the end of the war, the ground became a storage depot for the Ministry of Works, as well as a colliery training centre for 'Bevan Boys'. As for the conflict itself, it would cost the lives of two Swinton men, Tommy Holland (pictured left) and Richard Green (centre). Ironically, the men were close friends, having both been signed from Wigan Old Boys RUFC in the summer of 1932. Both are remembered on the cenotaph in Swinton town centre. The other player pictured is Gomer Hughes, who arrived at Station Road in 1934 from Penarth. Hughes would drink beer in extraordinary amounts, but this did not prevent him from winning the 1935 Championship with the Lions, or from playing for Wales 3 times. Sadly, his caps from Welsh Rugby Union were slower in forthcoming, since the Welsh RFU cynically withheld them because Hughes had signed for a Rugby League club. It was not until 1975 that they were posthumously awarded to his widow.

Immediately after the war, the Lions struggled to restore lost glories. Finishing twenty-fourth in 1946/47 represented a new low for Swinton, but even so, crowds remained reasonable. No less than 15,000 saw this 11-10 defeat by Wigan in January 1947.

Station Road continued to be well utilised for major events. On 12 October 1946, a crowd of 20,213 saw Wales surprisingly defeat England 16-13. Despite having a number of Welsh players on their books, not one Swinton player was involved – perhaps a sad indictment of the quality of the players brought north by the Lions. However, with the subsequent arrival from the valleys of Ralph Morgan, Frank Osmond, Bob Jones and Owen Phillips, this perception was rectified.

Between 1946 and 1958, Station Road hosted no less than nine Lancashire Cup finals. However, this perhaps emphasised the Lions' inability to reach major finals as much as their ground's appeal as a major venue. Wigan were successful in each of five finals between 1946 and 1951, the first of which was a 9-3 success over Belle Vue Rangers. The programme cover from the match was another striking design from the hand of Ernie Tynan.

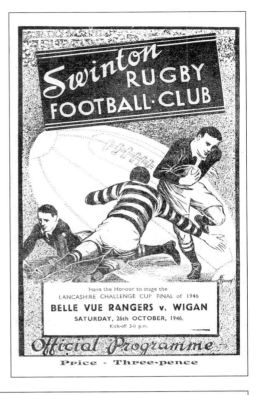

SWINTON RUGBY FOOTBALL CLUB

Have the Honour to stage the
LANCASHIRE CHALLENGE CUP FINAL of 1946
BELLE VUE RANGERS v. WIGAN
SATURDAY, 26th OCTOBER, 1946.
Kick-off 3-0 p.m.

Official Programme

Price - Three-pence

SWINTON FOOTBALL CLUB Co. LTD.

Tel. SWInton 1719

66, STATION ROAD, SWINTON,
MANCHESTER.

Date as Postmark

Dear Sir,

You are selected to play against *Workington*
at *Workington* on Saturday next.

~~Please meet on Ground~~ at ....

Bus leaves Town Hall, Swinton, at *8-0am*

Kick-off at *2-45 pm.*

If you cannot play, please notify me at once.

Yours faithfully,

SAM JONES, Hon. Secretary.

This selection confirmation card was sent to Swinton forward Harold Roughley in November 1946, prior to the long haul trip to visit new boys Workington Town. An eight o'clock departure for a 2.45 p.m. kick-off sheds some light on why a trip to Cumberland was a long, arduous and often unsuccessful task back in the 1940s.

On 10 March 1947, the Lions welcomed French visitors for the only time in their history. The Swinton line-up, from left to right, back row: Billy Williams, Ken Winkworth, Harold Palin, Jim Syddall, Ken Turner, Ralph Morgan. Front row: Norman Hodgkinson, Alan Roper, Joe Warham, Jack Stoddart (captain), Fred Garner, Eddie Turner. (Missing, Jim Davies.) In the Carcassonne line-up was the legendary French international full-back, Puig-Aubert.

The match against the French Champions was only saved following a dramatic thaw at the end of the great freeze of the winter of 1946/47. This left the pitch looking like a bog. The conditions did not suit the running style of the French, and Swinton secured a 7-2 victory, thanks to a try by Jack Stoddart and two goals by full-back Ralph Morgan. Morgan was a former South Wales policeman who came to Swinton from Newport RUFC. He was an excellent full-back and a superb place-kicker. Whilst with the Lions, Morgan was capped 3 times for Wales, but he signed for Leeds in 1952 after losing his place to Albert Blan.

In the summer of 1946, it was hoped that the launch of the Swinton and Pendlebury Intermediate League, which was open to players between the ages of eighteen and twenty-one, would produce some good local talent. This is the earliest known team group of Folly Lane Juniors, taken after a local cup final at Station Road in April 1947. The author's father, Tom, is sat on the grass in the middle.

A bright spot amongst the dismal late 1940s was a victory over the touring New Zealanders in September 1947. Another classic programme cover was the order of the day. Welshman Viv Warry and Swinton-born Ken Winkworth, both centres, scored the tries, whilst Eddie Turner booted a goal as the Lions won 8-6 in front of a 12,148 crowd.

The Lions pose prior to the match against the Kiwis. From left to right, back row: Bob Jones, Ken Turner, Ron Tucker, Norman Hodgkinson, Joe Warham, Eddie Turner, Viv Warry. Front row: Billy Williams, Frank Osmond, Jack Stoddart, Ken Winkworth, Fred Garner, Billy Riley. Two of the key players of this Swinton team were undoubtedly the hooker, Frank Osmond, and the prop-forward, Jack Stoddart. Osmond followed Ralph Morgan from Newport and established a reputation as one of the finest hookers of his era. He toured Australia with Great Britain in 1950 and, between 1948 and 1952, he won 14 caps for Wales (a Swinton record). In 1956, he was awarded a much deserved testimonial. Local man Stoddart had first forced his way into the side in the mid-1930s and was made club captain after the war. When he retired at the end of the 1950/51 season, he had completed nineteen years with the Lions, during which time he had become the proud owner of 6 Cumberland caps, gained in a period spanning ten years either side of the war.

Action from a heavy defeat at Wigan's Central Park in September 1948.

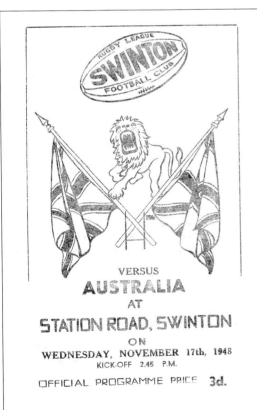

In November 1948, Swinton welcomed Australia to Station Road, defending a proud record against touring teams. Stretching back to 1911, the Lions had defeated Australia four times and New Zealand twice, suffering no losses. Colin Maxwell and Clive Churchill's 1948 tourists were, however, one of the finest ever to come to these shores, and they were to inflict a convincing 21-0 victory over an indifferent Lions outfit. A week earlier, a crowd of 36,354 for Britain's 16-8 success over Australia at Station Road represented the ground's record attendance for an international.

In December 1948, the Lions' long-serving secretary, Sam Jones, decided to call it a day. He had held the position for an astonishing forty-two years, and had even played on one occasion (in April 1907) during an injury crisis. His son, Vic Jones, took over as secretary, and he himself held the position for almost thirty years. Sam Jones died in 1958.

HALIFAX V SWINTON. R.L. CUP. MARCH 5TH 1949. 1 MINUTES SILENCE FOR D. CRAVEN.

March 1949 and Swinton line up in a blizzard, prior to a second round Challenge Cup match at Thrum Hall, Halifax. It looked to be heading for a 0-0 draw, but the Lions were sunk by a late drop-goal and last-minute try. From a lowly League position, the Yorkshiremen reached Wembley, whilst for Swinton, the curse continued.

74

Swinton players enter the field at Central Park in front of a 26,832 crowd, prior to a Lancashire Cup defeat at Wigan in September 1949. The season turned out to a good one, however, with the Lions surprisingly finishing third. The Lions had qualified for the top four by beating Salford 3-0 in front of a 20,000 Station Road crowd but, ravaged by injuries, they sadly lost their Championship semi-final, 9-0 at Huddersfield.

Station Road remained in demand for big matches. On 7 April 1951, the ground saw its record attendance, when 44,621 (larger than the population of Swinton itself) saw a dramatic last-minute try by Wigan's Brian Nordgren snatch a 3-2 victory and break Warrington hearts. However, the ground was certainly not full, and indeed, the Pendlebury Road end was later further banked up, leaving Station Road with a never-tested capacity in the region of 60,000.

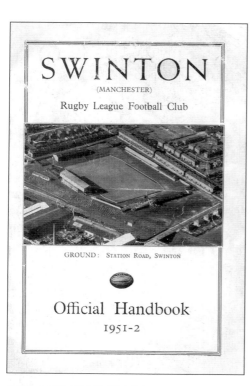

SWINTON
(MANCHESTER)
Rugby League Football Club

GROUND: STATION ROAD, SWINTON

Official Handbook
1951-2

This aerial photograph on the front cover of the 1951/52 official handbook shows Station Road at the height of its fame. 'The Barn' at the Station Road end of the ground had once stood on the popular side at Chorley Road, whilst the Townsend Road Stand had once provided the centrepiece of the old ground. The only new structure in Station Road's entire life-span was the main stand in front of the railway. Surrounding the entire circumference were massive open terraces. The Test match between Britain and New Zealand at Station Road in the autumn of 1951 was the first Rugby League match to be screened on national television by the BBC. The resumé is taken from the members' handbook for the 1952/53 season.

Post-War Years

The post-war years have been difficult ones for the Station Road Club. In the process of building, an abnormal number of player injuries and the terribly inflated market regarding new signings made the task exceedingly trying. They did, however, finish in the "first four" in the season 1949-50, being defeated rather narrowly by Huddersfield in the semi-final play-off game.

And To-day

TEAM BUILDING POLICY

Our policy has always been to encourage local talent, occasionally blended with outstanding players from the sister code.

How far have we gone during the past year or so in this direction? To name a few of recently signed young players of outstanding merit one turns to Albert Blan, Reginald Senior, Harold Lea, John Scott, Edward Billington, Peter Norburn, Cyril Moran, Russell Burn, Charley Armitt and there are several others. The future as regards playing strength is certainly an encouraging one.

Hardly a week passes but a new name is submitted; and in every instance our expenditionary force of scouts is on the *qui-vive* for recruits. Contrary to the belief in some quarters whilst we have not been able as yet to compete with some clubs in what has become a grossly inflated transfer market the Swinton club is continually making efforts to sign-on players that one day will bring back to Station Road the glories of the mid-twenties, when ALL the cups found a resting place there.

Ground Policy

Now let us turn to the ground policy. The Club has tried to provide an ideal location in the North for the Rugby League game. Even for club purposes there appears to be no reason why preparations should not be made to house the crowd which, it is hoped, ere long will assemble at an average match at Station Road.

Let us see what has happened since the Club decided to move from Chorley Road in 1929.

Since that date there have been no less than 25 representative matches staged on Swinton's ground at Station Road. Here they are :—

TEST MATCHES

Year	Match		Attendance
1930	Great Britain v. Australia	Attendance	33,809
1933	Great Britain v. Australia	,,	10,990
1937	Great Britain v. Australia	,,	31,724
1947	Great Britain v. New Zealand	,,	30,031
1948	Great Britain v. Australia	,,	37,169
1951	Great Britain v. New Zealand *	,,	29,104

*First Test Match to be televised. Estimated number of viewers 3,000,000.

INTERNATIONAL MATCHES

Year	Match		Attendance
1946	England v. France	Attendance	20,506
1946	England v. Wales	,,	20,213

Lancashire Cup Finals

Year	Match		Attendance
1930	St. Helens v. Wigan	Attendance	16,170
1933	Oldham v. St. Helens	,,	9,085
1935	Salford v. Wigan	,,	33,544
1939	Wigan v. Salford	,,	27,940
1947	Wigan v. Belle Vue R.	,,	21,648
1948	Wigan v. Warrington	,,	39,015
1950	Wigan v. Warrington	,,	42,240
1951	Leigh v. Wigan	,,	33,231

Challenge Cup Semi-Finals

Year	Match		Attendance
1930	Wigan v. St. Helens	Attendance	37,169
1933	Warrington v. St. Helens	,,	30,373
1934	Widnes v. Oldham	,,	17,557
1935	Castleford v. Barrow	,,	24,469
1946	Wigan v. Widnes	,,	36,976
1947	Bradford v. Warrington	,,	33,474
1948	Wigan v. Rochdale	,,	26,004
1949	Bradford v. Barrow	,,	26,900
1950	Wigan v. Warrington	,,	44,621

In addition there have been several County Matches staged at Station Road.

And on the 8th November next the ground has been selected for the 2nd Test Match : Great Britain versus Australia.

6

7

Arguably the most flamboyant Swinton player of the 1950s was Peter Norburn, who was signed in 1950 at the age of nineteen from the Worsley Boys Club in Wigan. He was five times the Lions' leading try-scorer and, with a career total of 166, only four other players have scored more tries for the club. He went on to gain 4 Lancashire caps and, on 28 November 1953, he was selected to play for England against the Other Nationalities, when he remarkably scored four tries. He was also selected for an Ashes decider against Australia at Station Road in 1956, but tragically had to withdraw because of injury. A test cap eluded Norburn thereafter, and he was also disappointed at missing out on the Great Britain tours of 1954 and 1958. By the time the Lions won back-to-back Championships in 1963 and 1964, Norburn had successfully made the transition from winger to second-row forward. He signed for Salford in 1964/65, having made 441 appearances for the Lions over fourteen seasons.

OFFICIAL PROGRAMME

PRICE
2d.

BLACKPOOL
RUGBY LEAGUE
SUPPORTERS' CLUB

——————— O F F I C I A L S ———————
VICE-PRESIDENTS:
ALD. J. PARKINSON
H. DOBSON, ESQ.
E. CROSS, ESQ.
A. JACKSON, ESQ.
J. SHEPHERD, ESQ.
R. W. BELL, ESQ.

S. C. ANDREW, ESQ., Chairman
F. GLEDHILL, ESQ. Hon. Secretary
P. GRIFFIN, ESQ., Hon. Treasurer
Thornton   Cleveleys   Branch:
J. CLANCY, ESQ., Chairman
HEADQUARTERS:
CLIFTON HOTEL
BLACKPOOL

Present

ROCHDALE HORNETS

versus

SWINTON

SATURDAY, 6th MARCH, 1954

KICK-OFF 3.0 P.M.

In March 1954, the newly-formed Blackpool Borough Supporters Club invited Swinton and Rochdale Hornets to put on an exhibition match ahead of Borough's application to join the League from the following August. Swinton lost, 10-8, before a crowd of 2,502.

Another Lion desperately unfortunate not to win a full Great Britain test cap was loose-forward Gordon Haynes, who came to Swinton from the Orford Tannery club in Warrington in 1953. He played for a Rugby League XIII against New Zealand in December 1955 and, the following March, he appeared for Great Britain against France at Odsal Stadium. However, as France were not awarded full Test status until the following season, a 'Test' cap was not forthcoming. After suffering serious knee problems, Haynes' career came to a halt at the end of the 1958/59 season.

Swinton line up with coach, Cliff Evans, prior to the start of the 1955/56 season. With his advanced training techniques and unique vision of the game, together with a superb youth policy, Evans would revolutionise fortunes at Station Road. Evans had replaced Griff Jenkins at the end of the 1953/54 season, after the Lions had finished in twenty-third position. From left to right, back row: Vic Jones (secretary), Arnold Thompson, Eddie Billington, Brian Greenhalgh, Tommy Holder, Les Woods, Peter Norburn, Alan Easterbrook, Eddie Cheetham, Gordon Haynes, Cliff Evans (coach). Seated: Cliff Berry, Gordon Hardman, Brian Critchley, Ken Winkworth, Albert Blan (captain), Jack Tobin, Hopkin Morgan, Frank Osmond, Tommy Mee (physiotherapist). Crouching: Albert Cartwright, Rees Thomas.

On 15 December 1956, minus the unfortunate Peter Norburn, Great Britain defeated Australia 19-0 at Station Road in order to win the Ashes series 2-1. This was the sixth time Australia had played a Test match at Swinton, and they were yet to register a victory.

Scrum-half Rees Thomas was a native of Maesteg, but came to the Lions from Devonport Services in 1949 after being released by the Royal Navy. Having only missed out on a full Welsh RU cap through appendicitis, he came north with a big reputation. He became a hugely popular player at Station Road and gained an unofficial Welsh cap in France in 1955, but with the emergence of Albert Cartwright, he was allowed to join Wigan. Whilst with the Central Park outfit, he won the coveted Lance Todd Trophy in 1958.

Boxing Day 1957, before a 24-0 success over Featherstone Rovers. Just a few weeks later, Rovers returned to Station Road to inflict a desperately disappointing defeat in the first round of the Challenge Cup. From left to right, back row: Peter Norburn, Ken Roberts, Jim Hope, Vinnie Smith, Gerry Doughty, Trevor Roberts, Harold Lamb. Front row: Cliff Berry, Lionel Robson, George Parkinson, Ken Gowers, Alan Worsley, Brian Critchley.

In front of a crowd of over 15,000, Swinton yet again bow out of the Lancashire Cup at the hands of Wigan, 30 August 1958. Here, winger Gerry Doughty (an England amateur international from Langworthy Juniors) struggles to evade a tackle.

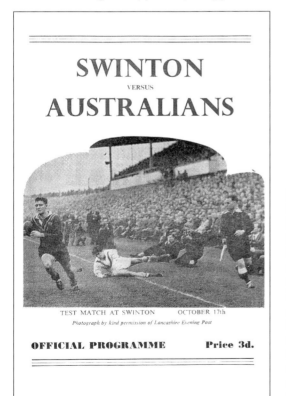

SWINTON

VERSUS

AUSTRALIANS

TEST MATCH AT SWINTON   OCTOBER 17th

Photograph by kind permission of Lancashire Evening Post

OFFICIAL PROGRAMME   Price 3d.

In 1959, the Australians returned to Station Road. On 17 October, the Aussies beat Great Britain for the first time on the ground by 22 points to 14, but against Swinton six weeks later, they had a remarkable escape. An Albert Blan hat-trick had helped Swinton to a single-point lead going into the last couple of minutes, and when the master tactician put Ken Roberts under the posts for a try, it looked all over. However, Roberts somehow failed to convert his own try. Australia immediately gained possession from the kick-off and went downfield to score a converted try to win 25-24.

Prior to the Australia fixture, the Lions' full-back Ken Gowers received an award from chairman Billy Scholes to mark his feat of breaking the club record for goals scored in a season in 1958/59. Gowers' tally was 116, but it was only two years before Albert Blan extended the record to 128 (which still stands). Other notable faces are those of ex-greats Bryn Evans, Tommy Armitt, Joe Wright and Martin Hodgson.

Peter Norburn throws his arms up to celebrate a try for Ken Gowers in Swinton's 25-5 thrashing of Salford at The Willows on 16 April 1960. Having finished sixth in 1958/59 and eighth in 1959/60, the Lions continued their steady improvement under Cliff Evans.

Three of Swinton's emerging stars, who would take the Lions to renewed glory in the early 1960s, were Ken Gowers, George Parkinson and Alan Buckley. Stand-off Parkinson made his debut as an eighteen-year-old in 1952 and, although his representative honours were restricted to just 4 appearances for Lancashire and one for the English Services, there was not a more respected player in the game. The most glowing tribute came from his coach, Cliff Evans, who remarked, 'I would say that George Parkinson is the finest covering half-back playing Rugby League today, and I cannot think of another stand-off who commands more respect from the opposition. He is strongly built, takes a lot of putting down in the tackle and there is no harder tackler than himself. An indomitable type of player and as hard as nails.' Parkinson was to play a crucial role in the Championship successes of 1963 and 1964, and left Swinton in 1966 after fourteen years' service.

In 1960/61, the Lions lifted their first post-war piece of silverware – the Lancashire League Cup. In the race for the overall championship, Swinton finished third and lost a semi-final play-off match at Warrington. The action shot here shows a try by Ken Gowers at Salford on 2 January 1961, in a match which Swinton won 24-5. Winger Johnny Stopford is also pictured.

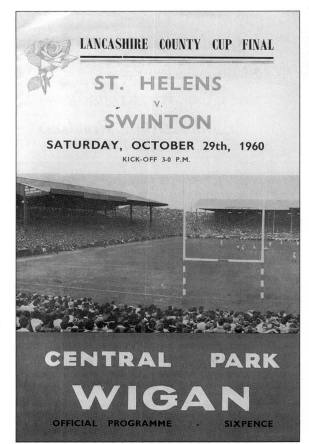

Swinton also reached the Lancashire Cup final for the first time in twenty years during 1960/61. Their opponents were St Helens, whom they would meet in similar circumstances three more times over the following four campaigns. Despite three goals from Albert Blan and a try by Ken McGregor, the Lions lost 15-9. In a repeat final twelve months later, Saints came out on top, 25-9.

Johnny Stopford (pictured centre against Wigan) was incredibly unfortunate to miss all four Lancashire Cup finals against St Helens through injury, and perhaps the lack of his scoring power was crucial in Swinton's ill-fortune – especially as one of his claims to fame was that he twice scored hat-tricks in direct opposition to Tom Von Vollenhoven. Stopford made his debut in 1958, and it was not long before he established a fearsome centre-wing partnership with the great Alan Buckley. Five times in six seasons, Stopford finished as the Lions' leading try-scorer, and his haul of 42 in 1963/64 remains a club record under Rugby League rules. A career total of 195 left him just two short of Frank Evans' overall record. Between seasons 1960/61 and 1965/66, Stopford gained 12 Great Britain caps, scoring 7 tries, and he also toured Australasia in 1966. Sadly, he died of cancer in 1998 at the age of sixty-two.

Action from a Swinton v. Wigan fixture in the early 1960s. The Lions' appropriately-named winger John Speed, who signed in 1960 from the Triangle Valve club in Wigan, takes on his opposite number.

Bobby Fleet was a Devon RUFC county centre when he was snapped up as a seventeen-year-old from Torquay in 1960. Here, he collects the ball with Wigan's Billy Boston in attendance. John Speed is to the right of the picture.

Action from Naughton Park in January 1962. Great Britain's Frank Myler is the Widnes player in possession. The Lions are (from left to right) Malcolm Cummings, Bernard McMahon and Peter Norburn.

Albert Blan came to Swinton from Wigan junior football in the summer of 1948, and quickly gained a reputation as a shrewd tactician. Signed originally as a goal-kicking full-back, he also enjoyed successful stints at stand-off, but it was his leadership from loose-forward that helped engineer two successive Championships for Swinton in the twilight of his career. Unjustly, he never received the recognition at representative level that his talents deserved. However, he did play for England against France in Paris during 1952/53, and he also gained 5 Lancashire caps over a period spanning ten seasons. Blan's last game for the Lions was at Halifax in the final fixture of the 1963/64 Championship campaign.

Swinton RLFC, 1962/63. From left to right, back row: Cliff Evans (coach), Derek Clarke, Ken Roberts, Malcolm Cummings, Dick Bonser, John Speed, Alan Buckley, Harold Bate, Ron Morgan, Ken Halliwell, Vic Jones (secretary), Graham Rees. Middle row: Peter Norburn, Bobby Fleet, Albert Blan (captain), Billy Scholes (chairman), Johnny Stopford. Front row: Albert Cartwright, Graham Williams, George Parkinson, Ken Gowers, Trevor Roberts, Frank Halliwell.

Having lost the previous two Lancashire Cup finals, the Lions again reached the final in 1962. However, yet again they lost to St Helens at Central Park – this time by a scoreline of 7-4. This was the one that got away, largely because George Parkinson had the ball knocked from his grasp by a goalpost in the act of 'scoring' what would have been a winning try.

Lions forward Ron Morgan gained a Great Britain cap in each of the club's Championship-winning seasons. He had previously been a Welsh international trialist during his time with Ebbw Vale RUFC. However, in the 1962 Lancashire Cup final, he was sent off following this incident (left) with Saints' Jack Arckwright. Making the tackle are John Speed, Peter Norburn and Trevor Roberts.

A muddy Station Road sees action between Swinton and Wigan at the end of the 'Big Freeze', 9 March 1963. The Lions lost 9-0, which left them perilously close to the relegation zone, but they suddenly hit a remarkable run of form. Their next match was drawn against Hull, then the final 17 fixtures were all won to leave the Lions Champions by 6 clear points. The inspiration had undoubtedly come from an unchanged and dazzling back-line of Gowers, Speed, Fleet, Buckley, Stopford, Parkinson and the former Folly Lane scrum-half, Graham Williams.

First Division Champions, 1963. From left to right, back row: John Speed, Alan Buckley, Peter Norburn, Albert Blan (with trophy), Ron Morgan, Harold Bate, Derek Clarke. Front row: Ken Gowers, Bobby Fleet, Johnny Stopford, Malcolm Cummings, Graham Williams, George Parkinson. The Lions had just beaten their long-time nearest rivals, Widnes, 22-4.

The Lions are accorded a civic reception at Swinton Town Hall. At the entrance are Jim Hope (the 'A' team captain, with the Lancashire Combination Trophy), Cliff Evans, the Mayor and Mayoress of Swinton & Pendlebury, and Albert Blan.

The trophies are displayed for the crowd from the Town Hall balcony.

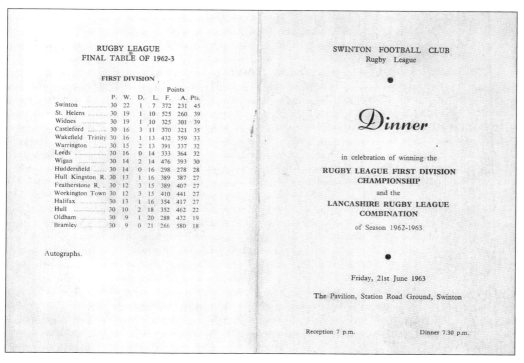

RUGBY LEAGUE
FINAL TABLE OF 1962-3

FIRST DIVISION

	P.	W.	D.	L.	F.	A.	Pts.
Swinton	30	22	1	7	372	231	45
St. Helens	30	19	1	10	525	260	39
Widnes	30	19	1	10	325	301	39
Castleford	30	16	3	11	370	321	35
Wakefield Trinity	30	16	1	13	432	359	33
Warrington	30	15	2	13	391	337	32
Leeds	30	16	0	14	333	364	32
Wigan	30	14	2	14	476	393	30
Huddersfield	30	14	0	16	298	278	28
Hull Kingston R.	30	13	1	16	389	387	27
Featherstone R.	30	12	3	15	389	407	27
Workington Town	30	12	3	15	410	441	27
Halifax	30	13	1	16	354	417	27
Hull	30	10	2	18	352	462	22
Oldham	30	9	1	20	288	432	19
Bramley	30	9	0	21	266	580	18

Autographs.

SWINTON FOOTBALL CLUB
Rugby League

Dinner

in celebration of winning the

**RUGBY LEAGUE FIRST DIVISION
CHAMPIONSHIP**

and the

**LANCASHIRE RUGBY LEAGUE
COMBINATION**

of Season 1962-1963

Friday, 21st June 1963

The Pavilion, Station Road Ground, Swinton

Reception 7 p.m.   Dinner 7.30 p.m.

A celebration dinner was held at the ground in June 1963, and this booklet was produced in commemoration. The League table displays the conclusive extent of the Lions' success.

In August 1963, Swinton set about defending their Championship with an excellent 16-4 victory over Wigan at Station Road. Derek Clarke, Albert Blan, John Speed and Bobby Fleet are in the thick of the action.

Throughout the 1960s, the Holy Grail for the Lions was unquestionably to reach Wembley and the Challenge Cup final. In 1964, fate appeared to deal another blow when Swinton were drawn away at Wigan in the first round, but a 15-15 draw was secured before a 31,752 crowd, which brought the Riversiders back to Station Road for a replay. Here, Johnny Stopford saves a try, with Ken Gowers looking on anxiously. On the following Wednesday, the Lions' club record attendance of 26,891 saw a sensational 13-8 victory for Swinton. However, it all went wrong in the quarter-final when, for the second season in succession, Widnes went through in a second replay.

The Championship was duly retained and again it was by 6 clear points, this time from Wigan. The celebrations are led by, from left to right, back row: Ken Halliwell, Barry Simpson, Peter Norburn, Frank Halliwell, Bobby Fleet, Malcolm Cummings, Ron Morgan, Albert Cartwright. Front row: Graham Rees, George Parkinson, Albert Blan (captain), John Speed, Graham Williams, Ron Morgan, Alan Buckley.

**RUGBY LEAGUE
FIRST DIVISION CHAMPIONS
1962/63**

SWINTON

VERSUS

WIDNES

Wednesday, 29th May, 1963.   *Kick-off 7-00 p.m.*

OFFICIAL PROGRAMME   **Price 3d.**

Two match programmes which proclaim the Lions' back-to-back title triumphs.

**RUGBY LEAGUE
FIRST DIVISION CHAMPIONS
1962-63 : 1963-64**

SWINTON

VERSUS

WAKEFIELD T.

Saturday, 23rd May, 1964   Kick off 3-00 p.m.

OFFICIAL PROGRAMME   **Price 3d.**

A team group from 1964/65. From left to right, back row: Barry Simpson, Ken Halliwell, Dave Robinson, Harold Bate, Graham Rees, Derek Clarke. Front row: Albert Cartwright, Frank Eckersley, Bobby Fleet, Ken Gowers (captain), Alan Buckley, Billy Davies, Johnny Stopford.

During 1964/65, the Lions reached the Challenge Cup semi-final. Successes over Dewsbury Celtic and Featherstone Rovers, then a titanic 8-6 victory at Wilderspool against Warrington, suggested that this was going to be the Lions' Wembley year at last. In the last four, they met Wigan at Knowsley Road, St Helens, before a crowd of 26,658. Swinton had already defeated Wigan twice in the League but, on the big occasion, they froze. Despite scoring first, the Lions eventually went down convincingly, 25-10.

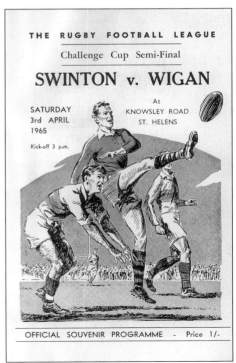

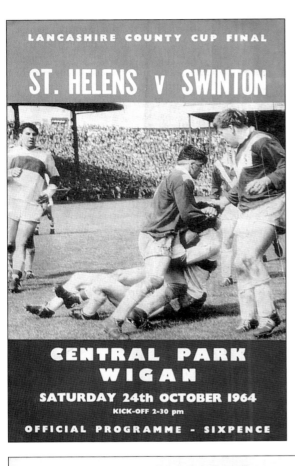

LANCASHIRE COUNTY CUP FINAL

ST. HELENS v SWINTON

CENTRAL PARK
WIGAN

SATURDAY 24th OCTOBER 1964

KICK-OFF 2-30 pm

OFFICIAL PROGRAMME - SIXPENCE

In October 1964, Swinton reached their fourth Lancashire Cup final in five seasons, but, yet again, they come out second best against St Helens, this time by a score of 12-4.

RUGBY LEAGUE FOOTBALL AT CENTRAL PARK, WIGAN

Lancashire Rugby League Cup—FINAL

ST. HELENS v SWINTON

SATURDAY, 24th OCTOBER, 1964

KICK-OFF 2-30 p.m.

Admit one New Stand	RESERVED SEAT	10/6
Row J Popular side entrance	Nº 48	Secretary
		Starrs of Wigan

Action from Station Road, *c.* 1965. Alan Buckley (ground) and George Parkinson make the tackle. The other Swinton players pictured are: Graham Rees, Ken Halliwell, Trevor Roberts, Dave Robinson, Malcolm Cummings and Johnny Stopford (number five).

In 1966, Lions full-back Ken Gowers received the accolade of 'Best and Fairest Player of the Season'. Here, he receives his trophy from Jack McNamara of the *Manchester Evening News*.

Great Britain's summer tour of Australia and New Zealand had a record four Swinton players in its ranks: Dave Robinson, Johnny Stopford, Alan Buckley and Ken Gowers. The series against Australia was lost 2-1, but New Zealand were defeated 2-0. Stopford played in the first Test against Australia, which was won, as well as 15 other tour games in which he scored 16 tries. Buckley played in three Test matches (missing the second Test against both opponents), whilst Gowers played in the deciding Test against Australia and both games against the Kiwis, kicking 14 goals in the process. Robinson, meanwhile, proved a great success, and the Swinton loose-forward played in all 5 Tests. The former Folly Lane amateur and Moorside school pupil gained 12 caps between 1965/66 and 1967/68, and was a great favourite at Station Road. However, in January 1970, he was controversially sold to Wigan for £10,000, although he did return briefly a few years later.

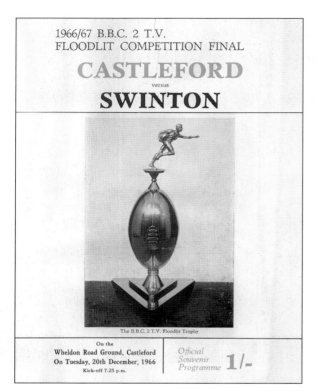

1966/67 B.B.C. 2 T.V.
FLOODLIT COMPETITION FINAL

CASTLEFORD

versus

SWINTON

The B.B.C. 2 T.V. Floodlit Trophy

On the
Wheldon Road Ground, Castleford
On Tuesday, 20th December, 1966
Kick-off 7.25 p.m.

Official Souvenir Programme **1/-**

The Lions reached the final of the BBC2 Floodlit Trophy in December 1966, but had to play the game on the ground of their opponents, Castleford. Despite a Man of the Match performance by Derek Whitehead, the Lions were defeated 7-2.

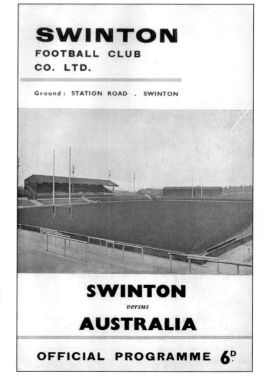

SWINTON

FOOTBALL CLUB
CO. LTD.

Ground: STATION ROAD . SWINTON

SWINTON

versus

AUSTRALIA

OFFICIAL PROGRAMME **6**D

On 22 November 1967, Swinton entertained an Australian touring team for what has since proved to be the last time. The Lions led 7-0 at one stage, but were eventually beaten 12-9. This left an overall record against the Kangaroos of 4 wins, a draw and 6 defeats (including 3 by a narrow margin) from 11 fixtures.

Desperate tackling from John Speed, Alan Buckley and Ken Gowers prevents a try at the Pendlebury Road end.

LANCASHIRE COUNTY
Challenge Cup Final

Leigh v. Swinton

at Central Park, Wigan
on Saturday, 1st November, 1969
kick off 3 p.m.

OFFICIAL PROGRAMME   ONE SHILLING

After a series of cup disappointments, the Lions finally got it right in the 1969 Lancashire Cup final, when Alex Murphy's Leigh were beaten 11-2. The star of the show was scrum-half Peter Kenny, who not only outwitted Murphy himself, but contributed four drop-goals to supplement a Mick Philbin try. The game took place at Central Park before a 13,532 crowd.

101

LANCASHIRE COUNTY CHALLENGE CUP - FINAL
AT CENTRAL PARK, WIGAN

LEIGH

versus

SWINTON

SATURDAY, 1st NOVEMBER, 1969

Kick-off 3-0 p.m.

10/-	Admit One	RESERVED
	New Stand	
W. JOHNSON		N? 111
Secretary	Row **D**	
	Popular Side Entrance	STARRS LTD.

Ticket for the Leigh *v.* Swinton game.

Swinton captain Bobby Fleet holds aloft the trophy whilst chaired by team-mates Harold Bate, Derek Clarke and Graham Mackay.

Coach Albert Blan lines up at Station Road with his successful Lancashire Cup squad. From left to right, back row: Harold Bate, Ken Gowers, Kevin Whittle, Graham Mackay, Bill Holliday, John Carey, Rod Smith, Derek Clarke, Albert Blan. Front row: Billy Davies, Alan Buckley, Peter Kenny, Mick Philbin, Billy Kearns (chairman), Bobby Fleet, John Gomersall.

Swinton inflicted another unexpected cup defeat on their Lancashire neighbours three years later, when, in defence of the Challenge Cup, Leigh were defeated 4-3 on their own ground. But there was heartbreak in the quarter-final at Halifax, when the Lions were beaten 9-8, thanks to a highly controversial last-minute penalty. Here, coach Dave Mortimer and kit-man George Jones dish out the beer to start the celebrations after the victory at Hilton Park.

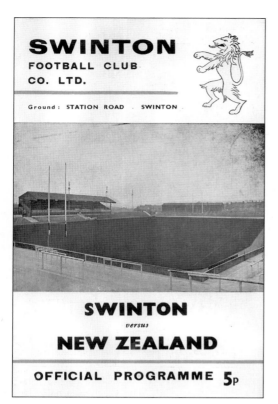

SWINTON

FOOTBALL CLUB
CO. LTD.

Ground : STATION ROAD . SWINTON

SWINTON

versus

NEW ZEALAND

OFFICIAL PROGRAMME 5p

8 October 1971 was the last time that the Lions entertained a touring New Zealand side and the Kiwis were sent packing, following a sensational match. Captained by Billy 'Daz' Davies (who, on 30 November 1968, had become the fifteenth and last Swinton player to be capped by Great Britain) and inspired by Ken Gowers and Peter Kenny, the Lions ran out 26-15 winners. Sadly for Swinton supporters, Davies would soon follow in the footsteps of Dave Robinson by joining Wigan for £10,000.

Players from Swinton and Oldham form a guard of honour as Ken Gowers makes his 601st and final appearance for the Lions in April 1973. Team-mate Alan Buckley and chairman Jack Bateman make the presentation. Gowers became the first Swinton player since Jim Valentine to be granted a second testimonial. This was also Swinton's last match of the one-division era, and, crucially, they failed to make the cut.

SWINTON
The Professionals Part 4

n last won the Lanca-
three years ago, when
t Leigh and although
ade several changes to
since then, they are
I they can do it again
noon.

ave a perfectly blended
youth and experience.
ury-hit Salford will
have all their work cut
p them.

BRILLIANT

back they are likely to
brilliant KEN GOWERS
just recovered from a
y. Gowers has won
natch with his excep-
al-kicking and Salford
to be wary of him this

right wing, will be the
OB FLEAY, who turned
al from Welsh Rugby
couple of seasons
HNNY COOKE, signed
a t l e y, and former
nal star, A L A N
form the centre
p, with former Salford

THE LIONS

SWINTON R.L.F.C. — 1972-73

Back Row (left to right): Mr. J. Bateman (Chairman), Frank
Hutton, Mike Doorey, John Cooke, Stan Gittins, Granville
Hoyle, Rod Smith, Bill Holliday, Steve Dainty, D. Mortimer
(Coach), V. Jones (Secretary). Front Row (left to right):
John Gomersall, Peter Kenny, Mike Philbin, Don Preston,
Albert Halsall (Captain), Alan Buckley, Dick Evans.

SWINTON FOOTBALL CLUB COMPANY LIMITED
Registered Office :
Station Road
Swinton

Directors: J. Bateman (Chairman), D. G. Jones (Vice-
Chairman), T. L. Green, R. Kenny, Dr. B. A. Sides, H. Edden,
J. H. Smith, J. S. Syddall, J. E. Thompson, W. A. Wallworth,
D. Mortimer (Coach), V. H. Jones (Secretary).

star PAUL JACKSON, on th
left wing.

COVER

Swinton have plenty of cove
at half-back. MICK PHILBI
and LES ATKINSON played las
week, but then there's PETE
KENNY, who missed the Hu
K.R. match last week because o
injury.

The Station Road side w
have a really powerful pack ou
—whatever the formation.

Forming the front-row shoul
be skipper ALBERT HALSAL
hooker DICK EVANS and th
powerful HAROLD BATE.

FORMATION

GRANVILLE HOYLE, BRIA
HEATON and ROD SMIT
formed the back three again
Hull K.R. but then B I L L
PATTINSON comes into th
reckoning today.

JOHN GOMERSALL and DO
PRESTON could also get a ru
out, especially if Heaton fails
recover from a damaged kne
But whatever the final line-u
this afternoon, Salford will kno
they've been in a match.

In October 1972, the Lions were defeated by Salford in the final of the Lancashire Cup at Warrington. The centre pages of the cup final programme reflect on Swinton's chances, but the Reds won comfortably, 25-11. The Lions would never again reach the final of this competition.

At the end of the 1972/73 season, Ken Gowers finally brought the curtain down on a Swinton career that had lasted nineteen years. After playing junior rugby in the Rochdale area, he had signed for the Lions in January 1954, and made his debut against Belle Vue Rangers the following November. He emerged as a full-back of consummate skill and impeccable positional sense, who also combined a deadly and accurate kick with resolute and perfectly-timed tackling. He was an integral member of the Swinton team which won the Championship in 1963 and 1964, but was controversially overlooked for the 1962 British tour of the Antipodes. However, he was selected in 1966, and, in all, gained 14 Great Britain caps (kicking 21 goals). Gowers also played once for England and picked up 12 Lancashire caps. 601 appearances, 970 goals and 2,105 points are club records that will surely never be beaten, whilst his tally of 12 goals against Liverpool City on 3 October 1959 is also a club record.

Alan Buckley brought his illustrious Swinton career to an end on 24 March 1974. In a career stretching back to 1959, when he had arrived from Broughton Park RUFC, the Lions centre had scored 192 tries (just 5 behind Frank Evans) in 467 appearances. Buckley was, of course, an integral member of the great Swinton side of the mid-1960s, and was a great maker of tries for his winger, Johnny Stopford, as well as a great scorer of tries himself, which he combined with almost ruthless tackling. He won 7 Great Britain caps (scoring one try), including 4 on the 1966 tour of Australasia, and was also the recipient of an England cap and 10 Lancashire caps. In 1971 he was granted a testimonial, but he became despondent at the Lions' fall from grace in the early 1970s and the ignominy of Second Division football prompted his retirement. He is pictured here with the 1969 Lancashire Cup.

The 1974/75 season threatened a brief revival in Swinton's fortunes. Both St Helens and Wigan were beaten in unbelievable John Player Trophy ties, whilst the Lions also swept to promotion to the First Division. The man at the coaching helm was Austin Rhodes, but he was to resign partway through the following season when Swinton chalked up just 6 League points and lost a record 20 consecutive matches.

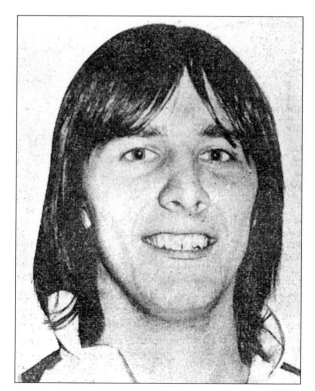

Tragedy struck on 3 March 1976 when Swinton winger Jeff Whiteside was critically injured during an 'A' team match at the Athletic Grounds, Rochdale. He died on 5 May.

Finishing fourth bottom of the Second Division with just 16 points in 1978/79 represented an all-time low for the Lions, but the appointment of Frank Myler as coach signalled a long-awaited revival. Here, he receives the Coach of the Month award for March 1980.

After Frank Myler and his assistant, Peter Smethurst, had controversially defected to Oldham, their successor, Tom Grainey, guided the Lions to the semi-final of the John Player Trophy in season 1981/82. Here, before a crowd of 6,728, Swinton attack the Salford line during an epic 6-0 quarter-final victory – a match which is fondly remembered in Swinton & Pendlebury.

The Lions' John Player Trophy performances earned them the title of Team of the Month for October 1981. Here, skipper Dennis Ashcroft receives the award.

Despite a superb performance by Swinton's sublimely skilled half-back, Alan Fairhurst, the Lions were defeated 23-14 by a strong Hull Kingston Rovers outfit in the semi-final. Apart from a 45-3 thrashing of Salford, which cost the Reds promotion, Swinton's League results were inconsistent. Tom Grainey was replaced by Jim Crellin in the autumn of 1983.

Danny Wilson was arguably Swinton's most talented player of the last thirty years. Arriving at Station Road in 1980, the twenty-four-year-old former Newport and Cardiff RUFC half-back was also the Lions' record signing. Wilson was simply a genius, capable of winning matches on his own with sheer skill that often bordered on the outrageous. That he remained at Swinton for the next eight years was due to his untamed maverick nature and 'off-field reputation', rather than any doubt that he could have performed at the very top level. Whilst with the Lions, Wilson picked up 4 Wales caps – on one famous occasion winning a Man of the Match award against England, despite being only half-fit.

Swinton returned to the top flight in 1985, after winning the Second Division Championship under Jim Crellin. To make matters even sweeter, promotion was secured with a 9-5 win at The Willows against Salford. Danny Wilson, Jeff Brown, Ken Jones (who scored two tries) and Derek Bate are pictured.

The celebrations are fully underway after the Championship was mathematically assured with a 44-8 victory over Rochdale Hornets on 17 April 1985. Jim Crellin and his assistant, Bill Holliday, can be seen on either side of the Championship Trophy.

Les Holliday receives a commemorative tankard from a fellow Cumbrian, the legendary Martin Hodgson, in order to mark the Lions skipper's selection for Cumbria against the all-conquering 1986 Australians. Holliday scored a try in a 46-12 defeat. The skillful ball-playing loose-forward was one of the Lions' finest and most popular players of the modern era. He was signed from Folly Lane in 1982, at the age of twenty, but a quest for honours saw him depart for Halifax in November 1987 for £65,000. He had further successful stints at Widnes and Dewsbury, before returning to the Lions in 1995. He later assisted Peter Roe before becoming Swinton coach in his own right, later being replaced by Mike Gregory.

Swinton's young team were ravaged by injuries during the 1985/86 season, yet only narrowly failed to remain in the top flight. The condemnation of the Townsend Road stand, and the need for expensive safety work in the aftermath of the Bradford fire, devastated the club's finances and scuppered plans to bolster the squad. Nevertheless, it was still a surprise when Jim Crellin suddenly resigned just before the start of the following season. From left to right, back row: Jim Crellin (coach), Norman Brown (physiotherapist), Andy Rippon, Tex Evans, Danny Wilson, Bill Holliday (assistant coach), Paul Topping, Mark Rowbottom, Alan Ratcliffe, Steve Walsh, Paddy Tuimivave, Terry Scott, George Jones (kitman). Front row: Tony Hewitt, Martin Lee, Mark Viller, Roby Muller, Les Holliday (captain), Derek Bate, John Allen, Gary Ainsworth.

Small consolation for their relegation came by way of an 18-16 victory in the Alliance Challenge Cup final against Leeds at Headingley. Captain Martin Lee lifts the trophy.

The Lions regained top-flight status in 1987, but had to settle for the runners-up spot behind Hunslet. However, revenge was gained in Old Trafford's inaugural Second Division Premiership final, when the same Yorkshire club was easily beaten 27-10. Here, Les Holliday celebrates with brother, Mike, and his coach and father, Bill.

Old Trafford, 17 May 1987. From left to right, back row: Mike Peers (joint coach), Joe Grima, Norman Brown (physiotherapist), Mark Viller, Alan Derbyshire (hidden), Steve Snape, Roby Muller, Martin Lee, Andy Rippon, Gary Ainsworth. Front row: John Allen, Les Holliday (captain), Jeff Brown, Derek Bate, Mike Holliday. Insets: Paul Topping and Alan Ratcliffe (who both left the pitch with broken legs).

Again, the Lions found life in the top division hard work and, once more, they were relegated. However, one success was Steve Snape, a centre signed in 1983 from local amateurs Folly Lane. Here, Snape shows pace to score against Hunslet in a 32-32 draw at Elland Road.

Controversy surrounded the appointment of Peter Smethurst as general team manager for the start of the 1987/88 season. Here, he is welcomed to the club for a third time by chairman Ian Clift, whilst 'A' Team coach Brian Robinson and first-team coach Bill Holliday look on. Despite his infectious enthusiasm, Swinton were relegated yet again and Smethurst resigned after an indifferent start to the following season's campaign.

Swinton's match against touring Papua New Guinea was sadly marred by demonstrations on the terraces directed towards Ian Clift and Peter Smethurst. However, an enjoyable game was won 13-6 before a crowd of 2,132.

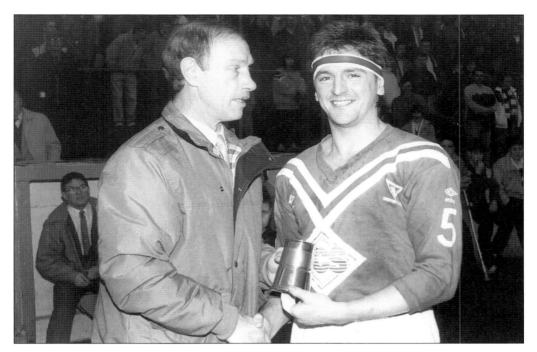

Swinton legend Alan Buckley makes a presentation to Derek Bate to mark the ex-Leigh Miners winger's 100th try for the Lions in January 1989. Bate was a prolific try-scorer, and his final tally for the Lions reached 119, including 32 in 1988/89 and 31 in 1986/87. In 1986, Bate equalled Jack Lewis' club record (set in 1900) of scoring in nine consecutive matches.

Stand-off Frank Cassidy was thrown in at the deep end following his arrival (along with his half-back partner, Tony Hewitt) from Wigan St Patrick's during 1985/86. He also recovered from a serious injury to win 2 caps for Great Britain Under-21s in 1988.

Despite only finishing in fifth place in 1988/89 under Frank Barrow, Swinton battled their way to the Second Division Premiership final following superb victories over York and Leigh. The final started well too, but, following the dismissal of prop-forward Steve O'Neill, it all fell apart. Here, Gary Ainsworth takes on the Sheffield Eagles defence at Old Trafford.

After Frank Barrow left to join St Helens as assistant coach, Swinton moved to re-appoint Jim Crellin, who had been sacked by Rochdale Hornets. Here, he lends a word of advice to the referee during a fixture against Halifax.

Joe Ropati makes a break against Fulham in November 1990. The Kiwi centre arrived at Station Road from Warrington with a reputation that he did not quite live up to, although he did help Swinton to yet another promotion under Jim Crellin in 1990/91. However, Crellin again resigned and was replaced by Australian player-coach Chris O'Sullivan. In turn, he was replaced by Tony Barrow in December 1991, when the club could not afford to honour his contract.

One of the Lions' most popular players throughout the 1980s and early 1990s was Alex 'The Little Beaver' Melling, seen here scoring a try against Dewsbury. The hooker made his debut in 1983/84, following his signing from Oldham St Anne's. Unspectacular, but efficient and reliable, Melling was the recipient of a well-earned testimonial in 1992.

The main entrance to Station Road, 1992. Swinton were relegated again, but this time it was accompanied by a financial disaster that resulted in the sale of Station Road for housing. Plans to relocate to Bury FC's Gigg Lane ground – made with no prior consultation with fans, businesses or the local council – were greeted with total disbelief and bitter anger from amongst the Swinton faithful. This was surely one of the greatest acts of treachery in British sporting history.

How did it come to this? The author of this book sits in the Swinton dugout with children Hayley and Stevie, contemplating the end of an era.

The Station Road ground, its terraces defiled by the contractor's bore holes, awaits its inevitable fate.

The scoreboard is still there for the time being, perched forlornly above the remains of one of the most famous rugby grounds in the world, as housing replaces the lush turf, August 1992.

Two-thirds of Swinton fans refused to travel to Gigg Lane in protest at the club's relocation. But after surviving liquidation and the launch of a new limited company (no thanks to Salford, Leigh and Wigan, who opposed their re-election to the RFL), the Lions soldiered on. Here, hooker Paul Gartland snatches a last-minute winning try against Huddersfield at Gigg Lane.

One of coach Tony Barrow's first signings after the move to Bury was former Wigan reserve-teamer Mark Welsby. Seen here scoring a try against Doncaster, Welsby was one of the finest full-backs outside the top division.

Another big success of the Gigg Lane years was winger Simon Ashcroft, who was recruited from Highfield in the summer of 1992. Although only slightly built, Ashcroft used considerable pace and his ability to break a tackle to score over 100 tries for the Lions.

Prodigal son Les Holliday returned to Swinton in 1995 for a final swan-song. In the first 'Super League' season of 1996, he captained the team to promotion from the Second Division and, after the dismissal of Peter Roe partway through the 1997 campaign, he took on the coaching role. He was subsequently replaced by Mike Gregory, after the Lions failed to make a realistic promotion bid to the Super League, despite heavy investment in players.

Kiwi stand-off Mark Riley became the first Swinton player ever to score 6 tries in a match on 11 August 1996. Prescot Panthers were the hapless team on the receiving end of a 90-0 drubbing, a score which also represented the Lions' biggest ever victory. Players who had achieved 5 tries in a match for Swinton were: Herbert Farr (1878), Jim Valentine (three times, twice in 1889 and again in 1893), Morgan Bevan (1898), Billy Wallwork (1900), Jack Evans (1922), Hector Halsall (1925), Dick Cracknell (1928), Randall Lewis (1946), Johnny Stopford (1962), Alan Buckley (1964), Joe Ropati (1990) and Jason Roach (in the same match against Prescot).

In the mauling of Prescot Panthers,
Australian Greg Pearce set another club
record by scoring 30 individual points,
made up of 11 goals and 2 tries. Bernard
McMahon's tally of 29 points against
Dewsbury in August 1959 comprised
(arguably a slightly more impressive)
10 goals and 3 tries.

Swinton Lions RLFC, season 1997. From left to right, back row: Andy Craig, Sean Casey,
Gareth Adams, Tony Barrow, Colin Armstrong, Leo Casey, Wes Rogers, Simon Ashcroft.
Middle row: Carl McCabe, Mark Welsby, Greg Pearce, Les Holliday, Steve Gibson, Mark
Sheals, Martin Birkett. Front row: John Gunning, Marlon Gardiner, Jimmy Evans, Peter Roe
(coach), Davide Longo, Peter Cannon, Mark Riley.

Mark Sheals, a local product from Folly Lane, enjoyed three spells with the Lions from the late 1980s through to 1997. He was the first Swinton prop-forward ever to score a hat-trick of tries in a game, and he presently holds the position of assistant coach.

The Challenge Cup draw in 1998 pitted the Lions against the Swinton amateur outfit, Folly Lane – the very same junior club that had provided the Lions with so many great players over the years. A crowd of 2,425, three times Swinton's average, turned out in a veiled protest at the club's relocation to Bury. Swinton won the game 74-6, but it was Folly Lane who took the applause at the end of the match. Here, centre Jimmy Evans goes over for one of the Lions' 14 tries.

One of the Lions' most exciting and promising young players of recent years was second-row forward Andy Coley. Unfortunately, he blotted his copy-book with the Swinton faithful by joining Salford Reds.

Failure to achieve promotion to Super League, the withdrawal of Super League cash, the realisation that Hugh Eaves had invested £440,000 that did not belong to him, and continuing dismal crowds at Gigg Lane, have all had a devastating effect on Swinton in the past couple of years. Certainly, coach Mike Gregory, the former Great Britain captain, did not have some of the financial advantages of his immediate predecessors. Gregory left at the end of the 2000 season and, sadly, matters came to a financial head in February 2002 when chairman and chief benefactor Malcolm White resigned his position at the club. However, with the likes of prop-forward Lee Hansen and hooker Rob Barraclough, the spirit of Swinton lives on. There are hopes that under new coach Phil Veivers, a former Australian star at St Helens, fortunes on the pitch will be revived.

1866

PRIDE IN THE LIONS

The Independent Swinton Supporters & Community Trust
70 Swinton Hall Road, Swinton, Manchester M27 4BJ
Tel: 0161 728 1068

www.lionstrust.co.uk

"for club and community"

A promotional brochure produced by the Swinton Supporters Trust. As a response to the club's serious financial position, the fans organised a Trust in the spring of 2002. All Swinton and Rugby League fans are now encouraged to get involved in this democratic co-operative movement, which intends to help to safeguard the club's future by investing in it, and receive a shareholding and seats on the board of directors in return. The Trust has already been instrumental in helping to bring the club back nearer to its roots, following the announcement of a ground-sharing arrangement with Salford City FC at their Moor Lane ground and improvement in its links with the community via local amateur clubs, schools and general awareness programmes. For more information concerning the organisation, please note the contact points stated on the cover of the brochure.